To

Mr. A. J. Eken

and

Mr. A. J. Eken Jr.

with The complements of

George Adams

Dartmouth 1905

THE STORY OF DARTMOUTH

President's House
Frontispiece

THE STORY OF DARTMOUTH

BY
WILDER DWIGHT QUINT

WITH ILLUSTRATIONS BY
JOHN ALBERT SEAFORD

BOSTON
LITTLE, BROWN, AND COMPANY
1922

Copyright, 1914,
By Little, Brown, and Company.

———

All rights reserved

378.742

Qu

LD

1438

Q5

Printed in the United States of America

PREFACE

I HAVE to acknowledge gratefully my indebtedness in writing this " Story of Dartmouth " to the remarkable " History of Dartmouth College, Volume I," by the late Frederick Chase, and the equally excellent " History of Dartmouth College, Volume II," by John K. Lord.   Other useful and interesting material I have found in the Rev. Francis Brown's " Origins of Dartmouth College; " Professor Charles F. Emerson's historical sketch introductory to the Dartmouth General Catalogue of 1911; " The Dartmouth Roll of Honor," by Redington and Hodgkins; " Dartmouth Athletics," by John H. Bartlett, '94; Dr. W. T. Smith's " Hanover Forty Years Ago; " Crosby's " First Half Century of Dartmouth College " and various letters, diaries, and magazines.

W. D. Q.

October 1, 1914.

27376

CONTENTS

LIST OF ILLUSTRATIONS

THE
STORY OF DARTMOUTH

CHAPTER I

" THE INDIAN CHARITY SCHOOL "

ON the evening of February 6, 1766, an oddly
assorted pair of Americans reached London,
the great Babylon of its day, after a seventeen-hour
coach ride from Salisbury. Since the twenty-third
of December, the two had been on their journey
from Boston, in the far-away colony of Massachusetts. Neptune and Aeolus had played them scurvy
tricks. Their passage in the ship *Boston Packet*,
Captain John Marshall, toward the cost of which
John Hancock, one of the ship owners, had remitted
five pounds, had been sufficiently trying to men of
little marine experience; to add exasperation to
physical ill-being, an easterly gale had kept them
from port for twenty-two days, and within two
hundred miles of Land's End. But on February 3
they were landed at Brixam in a fishing-boat.

By horses' backs and coaches they made their

1

way to the metropolis, reaching it when oil wicks were guttering in the street lamps, and torches flaring as the link-boys rushed hither and thither, like the saucy young imps of darkness they were. That the travelers from America were confused, startled, and astounded may be taken for granted, but need not be; their letters and diaries give notable testimony to the perturbed state of their feelings at being projected into London life for the first time.

These men could and did attract the attention of the London crowds, even at a time when it was the fashion to pretend a cool indifference to anything but the doings of the " Macaroni." Samson Occom, the older of the two, was a full-blooded Mohegan Indian from Connecticut. With his lithe, athletic figure, his strong, copper-tinted face, his straight black hair hanging over his shoulders, his broad, white bib-tie and sober clerical clothes, he made a picture of contradiction that caught the eye of serious and frivolous alike.

Occom's companion, Nathaniel Whitaker, was tall, handsome, and distinguished in bearing. He, too, was a man of God of that robust and somewhat quarrelsome type that New England produced so prodigally in the seventeenth and eighteenth centuries. He was a Princeton College Presbyterian, and destined later to raise his voice in fiery denunciation of Toryism; to squabble with his people in every pastorate he held; to be accused of trying to "corner" the wine and raisin market in Norwich, Connecticut, while a pastor there, and to be called by the historian of that town "a worldly man and frequently irregular." Possibly the Reverend Mr. Whitaker was a too-jaunty shepherd for Puritan flocks; but his qualities certainly gave him efficiency for his London mission.

Samson Occom, "the glory of the Indian nation," and Nathaniel Whitaker, of more doubtful glory, had come to London to stir up subscriptions for the "Indian Charity School," located in Lebanon, Connecticut, and the direct ancestor of Dartmouth College. This institution was owned and conducted by Eleazar Wheelock, Yale 1733, already a noted pulpiteer, pamphleteer, controversialist, and educator. The pilgrims were accredited to George Whitefield, that flaming sword of Zion, who knew Wheelock well and was eager to help him in his great plans for educating and then Christianizing the young savages of the eastern border of America. As a matter of fact — though they themselves could not have known it — they were on their way to the highly respectable and God-fearing nobleman who was to give his name to the collegiate child of

Eleazar Wheelock's mind and heart. After Wheelock, the "Great Awakening," the American Indian,
and the British peerage formed the trio most influential in the founding of Dartmouth.

These American ambassadors from the learned
Connecticut parson and school-teacher spent their
first somewhat disturbed night in London at the
house of Dennis De Berdt, a rich merchant who
had been in correspondence with Wheelock through
Whitefield's influence. The next morning they
were taken to the house of the revivalist, afterward
being provided with a furnished house hard by the
Temple through his generous effort for their comfort.

Evidently Whitefield had long held prophetic
vision of the Earl of Dartmouth as one who would
listen to the Macedonian call from Wheelock and
his Indians; that if he would not go over and help
them, he would at least provide some of the sinews
for the holy war and induce others to do the same.
The Americans had been in London hardly a week
before he arranged a meeting with the peer, who was
at that time First Lord of Trade and Plantations
and afterward (1772) Secretary of State for the
Colonies. Says Occom in his diary: "Monday,
Febru' 10th, Mr. Whitefield took Mr. Whitaker
and I in his Coach and Introduced us to my Lord

Dartmouth, and he apear'd like a Worthy Lord indeed Mr. Whitefield says he is a Christian Lord and an uncommon one." [1]

But Occom's naive approval of the second Earl of Dartmouth did not extend to Londoners *en masse*. "Last Sabbath Evening," continues the diary, " I walk'd with Mr. Wright to Cary a letter to my Lord Dartmouth and Saw Such Confution as I never dreamt of, there was some at Churches Singing p'g and Preaching, in the Streets Some Cursing, Swearing and Damming one another, others was holloaing, Whestling, talking, gigling, and Laughing, and Coaches and footmen passing and repassing, Crossing and Cress-Crossing, and the poor Begers Praying Crying and Beging up on their Knees."

Of the two, Whitaker was the more practised man of the world. It is not on record that any of the sights of London, either sacred or profane, hurt his sensibilities in any way. He knew that his mission was to raise money, and he realized the

---

[1] That closing statement, while evidently written in sober earnest by the Indian minister, was the cause of tremendous hilarity when quoted by Professor Francis Brown in his address, *The Origins of Dartmouth College*, at the proceedings incident to the laying of the cornerstone of the new Dartmouth Hall, October 26, 1904. The sixth Earl of Dartmouth, who was seated on the platform, was the first to see the joke, and his roars of laughter belied the reputation of his countrymen as to quick appreciation of humor.

5

value of a friend in high places. With all his apparent lack of tact — Whitefield termed him "forward," but admitted that he was "certainly very indefatigable" — he was a good promoter and doubtless knew something of the science of advertising, since Occom soon became quite the rage in London, where he was mimicked on the stage. The Mohegan preacher "little thought," he wrote, "I should ever come to that honor." But if the ungodly played upon his fame, the godly did something to atone therefor by naming a popular new hymn-tune *Lebanon* in honor of his American place of residence, and by singing his own hymn, *Awaked by Sinai's Awful Sound*, which is still in use in some of our church collections.

Lord Dartmouth's favor having been won, together with an initial subscription of fifty pounds for the Indian Charity School, the road to success was well opened. Under date of March 19, 1766, Whitaker wrote to Wheelock:

"Mr. Whitefield is entirely friendly, and by his friendship I have my Lord Dartmouth's, so our way to the throne is very short. The kg. hath not seen Mr. Occom as yet because of this plagy stamp act. But now thats all over I expect he will see him as soon as Mr. Occom is well of ye smallpox, which tis likely will be in 8 or 10 days. The K. has promised £400–*tace*, when this is done and comes to be known; then the carnal Presbyterians will be obliged to follow, as well as the Church folks."

The king finally gave two hundred pounds, and there is a poetically pleasing, but unconfirmed tradition that Occom preached before the royal George. However, it is known that the Indian and his clerical manager met the Archbishop of Canterbury, who then seemed friendly enough, though he afterward observed that " as the Dissenters did not help us, neither will we help them," and the Bishop of Gloucester, who, as Whitaker notes, " would not give us a penny nor ask us to sit down!" As a matter of fact, the hostility of the established church toward the Connecticut enterprise grew marked as time went on.

But Dartmouth's patronage was powerful enough to overcome many sneers and even threats by others. With it came the interest of Robert Keen, a woolen-draper who was generous to the cause, and John Thornton, a rich Clapham merchant, whose portrait, now in possession of the college, presents a perfect picture of the bluff, stormy, big-hearted father of the Old Comedies.

Thornton was an eccentric genius, with a penchant for giving away money that would have brought a less wealthy man to the almshouse. He would lend large sums to young tradesmen without security; he would amuse himself by buying church livings and making gifts of them to struggling clergymen; he would publish religious books at his own expense and send them all over the world in his ships. To a man of his temperament, the Indian Charity School idea, with its substratum of religious prose-lyting, must have appealed strongly. The redskin preacher, who was so great a factor in the money-raising because " he was himself the embodiment of his cause," was a better argument for Thornton than a dozen polished exhorters could possibly have been.

Occom's activity, doubtless kept warm by Whit-aker's superior energy and sense of publicity values, was extraordinary. During their stay in Great Britain, he preached over three hundred sermons, and so well did he comport himself in the pulpit that he aroused visions of a great conversion of the Indian race. He had something of the redskin's native eloquence and imagination, and he was practical enough to know that he wanted money and to ask for it. Contributions flowed in. All sorts and conditions of men and women, from the throne to the peasant's farmhold, gave to this strange, new cause. There were twenty-five hundred names on the final list, and not the least appealing to the Dartmouth of to-day are the entries: " A Widow, 5s " and " Two Widows, 10s. 6d." [1]

Before coming across the sea on their quest of gold, Whitaker and Occom had been warned of the not too Christian animosities that lay between the two great missionary societies of London and of Edinburgh, " The Society for the Propagation of the Gospel in Foreign Parts " and " The Society in Scotland for Propagating Christian Knowledge." Wheelock had received money from each for his Lebanon school and had diplomatically kept peace between their Boston branches. It was Whitaker's business to do the same in England, and he seems to have been fairly successful. Even Whitefield counseled deception; Whitaker must wholly dis- avow any connection with the Scotch Board, for Lord Dartmouth himself " would by no means lift for it " — and he did it like a gentleman while below the Scottish border.

In Scotland, where the two later made a success- ful tour, it was a different story. At Edinburgh, the Scotch Society made a proposition to assume the complete patronage of the Indian Charity School, promising more subscriptions if Wheelock

---

[1] Among the earlier gifts in America to the Indian Charity School was one marked as coming from Benedict Arnold, Esq., amounting to " a large proportion of the profits of a venture which he sent to sea."

would give up the English allegiance. Wheelock's worldly sense thought the scheme " worth considering, as perhaps we can control both, and so have two strings to the bow." The Scotch Society did, in fact, become the trustee of the collections made in Scotland, and to this day has a fund for " clothing, boarding and maintaining such Indians as are designed for missionaries and schoolmasters " at Dartmouth, which moneys they do not know how to use.[1]

After the Scotch tour, the two propagandists thought of Ireland as a fertile field for their labors, and went across the channel. But here Whitaker found that for once he had been overreached in enterprise, and that one Morgan Edwards was there gathering in the pounds and shillings for a " Baptist college to be set up in Rhode Island " (afterward Brown University). Whitaker honorably left the ground to his predecessor, and he and his protégé returned to England by the next ship.

In truth, neither Wheelock nor the friends of the Indian Charity School had any cause to complain of the results thus far attained. By the autumn of 1766, the English fund amounted to five thousand

---

[1] The last Indian graduate of Dartmouth was Charles A. Eastman, of the class of 1887, the Sioux who is now well known as a physician and author.

pounds, a goodly sum for that day. So goodly was it that many of the donors began to grow restless. How was it to be administered and by whom? Was a man in distant America, whom not one of them had ever seen, to be given control of so much? Who knew that Whitaker would turn it over intact to Wheelock. The demand for a board of trustees began to be heard. At first neither Lord Dartmouth nor Whitefield favored the plan. They had implicit faith in Wheelock and believed that all the money should be placed in his hands, he to make immediately a will that should provide for the fund's use in the event of his death and for naming of a successor. " You must immediately make your will and fix your Successor, to give him the monies in trust for the School," Whitaker sent word to him.

Wheelock wrote that this was satisfactory, and that he would name Whitaker as his Elisha. It was probably a happy circumstance that the mantle was not so to fall. Whitaker's subsequent career was not such as to suggest a very pleasing picture of him as president of Dartmouth College, although he might have been the cause of no more trouble than was Wheelock's own son, as will appear later.

However, the trusteeship scheme won ground rapidly. In June, Whitaker, who scented the coming bondage, wrote to his chief: "A charter is not necessary — the most of the Societies here are self-formed and yet some have very large funds, yet I will try to obtain a charter, if friends will agree — but I know you will object that it will tie your hands. The Serious here are sick of trusts."

The last sentence has a curiously modern sound. The "Serious" are still with us.

Returning to London from a tour of the western counties of England, which proved to be a comforting money-getter, Whitaker and Occom found that the trust had been arranged and its nine members chosen. Lord Dartmouth was president; the jovial plutocrat, John Thornton, was to handle the finances, and Robert Keen was to be the secretary. It was a strong board, hardly to be bettered throughout the whole of England in its neat balance of varied humans and their diverse influences. Whitaker surrendered to it at once, as indeed he knew he must, and Wheelock a little later, though with many pangs, for he feared that the absent treatment his little institution might receive from trustees thousands of miles away might make his work futile. But he knew when to yield diplomatically. "The gentlemen of ye Trust," he wrote to Whitaker, November 28, 1767, " shewed a laudable and Christian Integrity toward ye Redeemer's cause as ye matter appeared to them — I never blamed them so much as in a tho't."

The work of the Mohegan minister and his tireless protector was now nearing its end. The freshness of Occom's personal appeal was wearing away, and there were signs that the movement was going stale. Unfortunately, too, the almost inevitable scandal accompanying the raising of educational funds in those days made its appearance here. It came from a misunderstanding, but had an ugly look for a time. It appears that Wheelock, believing that the disposal of all the moneys collected would be by his own hands, had written Whitaker early in 1766:

You are hereby empowered to remit in goods, to the amount of two or three thousand pounds lawful money, for the Supply of the Indian Charity School under my care and for the missionaries, from time to time, upon the credit of the donations given in Europe for that purpose, and to assure the merchants of whom you have said goods, that upon your advice of them I will draw orders upon persons in whose hands the donations are for the payment of the same.

That seemed fair and well; the trouble was that the trustees, when they came into power, were not informed of the plan. Opening some letters to Whitaker from a Mr. Eells, a friend and co-worker of Wheelock's, they found various mention of this plan. They at once thought they scented a swindle, dishonored one of Wheelock's drafts that came over about that time, and sent him this stinging rebuke:

MR. ELEAZAR WHEELOCK.

REV. SIR, — We must acknowledge we have been very much alarmed at finding some clandestine dealings betwixt the Rev. Mr. Eells, of Stonington, and Mr. Whitaker, which had we been apprised of, we should have declined accepting the trust; and we consider it in such an iniquitous light that if it is not put a stop to, we shall decline acting any further as trustees for your school; which we desire therefore you would see immediately done, and then we shall rejoice to give you all the assistance we can.

Even the faithful Whitefield was furious.

"I think the scheme concocted with Mr. Eells very iniquitous and exceedingly imprudent," he wrote to Wheelock. "How came you to draw so many hundreds this last year, and why no account of the disbursements? I hope no money is lodged in traders' hands. If it is, it must be drawn out, expended and accounted for, before any more is transmitted."

Wheelock, acknowledging that the thing looked "shocking" in its nakedness, was able to dress it with such reasonable explanations that the trustees were satisfied with his honesty. They continued to mistrust Whitaker, however, and demanded that Wheelock change his will, cutting out the suspected parson from the succession and bequeathing everything to the board of trustees in England, which was to have a veto power over an American board of eight.

Under the lash of necessity Wheelock acquiesced. He writhed, for he had not the meekness of a proverbial Moses; but his yielding was in the end a blessing. And it is but fair to the English trustees to say that they were ever sensible, liberal, and decent toward Wheelock during the whole life of the trust, which ended in 1775, when the collections were all expended. Lord Dartmouth, if perhaps regarded as something of a prig by the roaring, stout-drinking, fox-hunting types of the British nobility of his time, was a gentleman and a good friend of America. He doubtless influenced the other members of the board to fair treatment of the Charity Indian School and its somewhat irascible preceptor.

In April, 1768, the Charity School collectors sailed for home, arriving at Boston in eight weeks. They had easier weather, and their spirits were high. No wonder. In their two and a half years' pilgrimage they had been instrumental in getting together for the glory of God and the conversion of the Indian over eleven thousand pounds. No school in America had ever won so handsome an amount in England. Wheelock's confidence in the drawing power of Occom had been justified. His first pupil had paid his debt many times over.

CHAPTER II

THE EVOLUTION

WHILE Samson Occom and Nathaniel Whitaker were tapping the English rocks and bringing forth such pleasing streams of gold for the Indian Charity School, Eleazar Wheelock was wrestling mightily with the angel of discontent, despite the fact that he had turned out some very fair specimens of Anglicized and Christianized Indians. One of these was Joseph Brant, the great chief of later days and one of the ablest redskins civilization ever produced. Others were Joseph Woolley, David Fowler, and Hezekiah Calvin, all three of whom had been sent out as missionary-teachers to the Mohawks. They had the valuable favor of Sir William Johnson, that picturesque Irishman who lived in baronial style at Johnson Hall in the Mohawk Valley and became a quasi-lord of the manor to the Indians of the Six Nations by reason of his tact, his fairness, and his infinite knowledge of their language, thoughts, and habits.

17

THE STORY OF DARTMOUTH

In October, 1765, Wheelock's "boys" in the field had one hundred and twenty-seven pupils all told. One of Wheelock's white pupils, Samuel Kirkland, who was to be the father of a president of Harvard College, was already with the Oneidas and doing splendid service — so splendid that Wheelock seems to have been jealous of his rising fame, and at one time feared that the English board would have been pleased to oust him from control of the Charity School funds in favor of his young graduate.

Wheelock saw with uneasiness that the Indian teachers had not been so successful and that they were not overmuch in love with their work. Fowler, writing from "Canavarohaie in Oneida," under date of June 15, 1765, thus aired his grievances:

This is the twelfth day since I began to keep my school, and I have put eight of my scholars into the third page of the spelling book. . . . I never saw children exceed these in learning. The number of my scholars is twenty-six, when they are all present, but it is difficult to keep them together; they are often roving about from place to place to get something to live on. Provisions are very scarce with them. I am also teaching a singing-school. They take great pleasure in learning to sing; we can already carry three parts of several tunes. . . . I have been treated very kindly since I came to this place. . . . My cooks are as nasty as hogs, — their clothes are black and greasy as my shoes, their hands are as dirty as my feet; but they cleanse them by kneading bread. Their hands will be clean after kneading three or four loaves of bread. I am obliged to eat whatever they give me, for fear they will be displeased with me. After this month I shall try to clean some of them, for I must move along by degrees. If I once get out with them, it is all over with me.

Wheelock was coming to realize that Indian was a poor mentor for Indian, and his dissatisfaction grew with several fresh reverses in the field. Though his training-school at Lebanon was prosperous enough, he felt that the work of the kingdom lay in the wilderness, and he saw that he was not getting results. He had sent to the Onondagas his oldest son, Ralph, who was now heir apparent by the terms of the will changed at the order of the English trustees. The fond father was singularly misguided as to the character of his son, who lacked everything that a missionary to the Indians should have had in the way of tact, forbearance, and a sense of justice, and who made redskin enemies faster than the elder Wheelock could make friends. Joseph Brant told a story of him that illustrates the point.

One day, according to Brant, Ralph brusquely ordered a Mohawk half-breed at the Lebanon school, William (Major) by name, and an illegitimate son of Sir William Johnson himself, to saddle his horse for him. William refused on the ground that he was not there for any such menial purpose, and that he was a gentleman's son.

" Do you know what a gentleman is? " sneeringly asked the young Wheelock.

" I do," promptly returned William, doubtless with the picture of his titled father in mind. " A gentleman is a person who keeps race-horses and drinks Madeira wine; and that is what neither you nor your father do. Therefore, saddle the horse yourself." For this retort courteous, Ralph induced Eleazar Wheelock to send William back to Johnson as " too proud and litigious." This did not tend to make the powerful lord of Johnson Hall any the more pleased with the Wheelocks, though he had for some time given them and their branch schools great help in his domain. He had safeguarded their native teachers and had even fed them from his stores. But his favor was rapidly being alienated.

Ralph Wheelock's last trip to the Onondagas was most disastrous. Upon his arrival, he found Kirkland ill and just departing for Connecticut, whereupon he bitterly attacked the missionary before an Indian council, calling him " no more than a servant of my father who is at the head of the ministers of New England and known beyond the

Rollins Chapel

Great Water." He pompously boasted: " When he dies, I shall succeed him and manage all the affairs of instructing the Indians."

The redskins were angered beyond measure, both because they hated Ralph and liked Kirkland. According to the narrative of " Indian Thomas ", this was their answer, delivered by a chosen orator:

Brother, we heartily thank you that we now understand the whole of your messages as you are come with the word of God. You have spoken exceedingly well, very sweet words indeed, as coming from the tongue from whence we perceive you have spoken. But, brother, do you think we are altogether ignorant of your methods of instruction? [Then taking and shaking him by the shoulder,] Why, brother, you are deceiving yourself! We understand not only your speech but your manner of teaching Indian. Brother, take care; you are too hasty and strong in your manner of speaking before the children and boys have any knowledge of your language. Why, brother, if another hears my dog barking, or having hold of a creature, and bids him get out and perhaps he don't obey him immediately, not understanding the voice. Upon which the stranger catches up a club and mauls my dog. I shall resent it, because he is my dog. Brother, I love my dog. What do you think of children, in like case?

Young Wheelock was " much affrighted ", says " Indian Thomas ", who asked the speakers to cease their shouting and yells of contempt. Finally, as quiet was restored, came this gravely significant remark from one of the tribe:

Brother, you must learn of the French ministers if you would understand and know how to treat Indians. They don't speak roughly, nor do they for every little mistake take up a club and flog them. It seems to us that they teach the word of God. They are very charitable, and can't see those they instruct naked or hungry.

Never from an Indian mouth was there a more pungent estimate of the difference between the methods of the domineering English and those of the suave, tactful French in the handling of the essentially proud men of the forests.

This was the last exploit of Ralph Wheelock in the rôle of *enfant terrible*, but it was sufficient to estrange Sir William Johnson still further. It is but just to the boy, however, to remember that even at this time he was subject to epileptic attacks, which later so wrecked his intellect that he was put under guardianship and even kept a prisoner at times. Disease shattered forever his dream of succession.

But the final blow to Eleazar Wheelock's hopes of establishing intimate Christian relations with the Six Nations was dealt by the inept hand of another of his emissaries. The story is picturesque.

In the summer of 1768, Wheelock, whose ears

were keenly attuned to the public sounds that might be of advantage to his enterprise, heard from some Oneidas who visited him at Lebanon, of a great council shortly to be held at Mount Johnson under the auspices of Sir William. All the tribes in this feudal lord's jurisdiction were to take part; presents and plenteous rum were laid in stock, for the intent was, as usual, to win something from the Indians at small cost — in this case land. The Connecticut pedagogue believed that in the general allotment he might be lucky enough to obtain a grant at a new location for his Charity School — he was by now despairing of any further advance in Connecticut. He decided to send an agent to the congress, and finally picked Reverend Jacob W. Johnson, of Groton. Never was choice of ambassador more unfortunate.

At Fort Stanwix more than three thousand Indians had gathered in their most splendid panoply. Their hosts, beside Sir William Johnson, were Governor Franklin of New Jersey, and Governor Penn of Pennsylvania, together with, according to Chase, " a number more of great and wealthy gentlemen from those provinces and from Virginia, with a great sum of gold and silver and numerous batteaux of blankets and other goods; their purpose being to obtain from the Indians the cession of a large tract of their lands under cover of a settlement of boundaries " — in other words to swindle them.

Upon his arrival at this extraordinary camp, Reverend Mr. Johnson immediately proceeded to attack the land cession scheme of the governors and plutocrats. He voted himself counsel for the Indians and did his utmost to stir up among them opposition to the plan. He " even had the face ", wrote Sir William to General Gage, " in opposition to his majesty's demands and the desire of the colonies to memorial me, praying that the Indians might not be allowed to give up far to the North or to the West but to reserve it for the purposes of Religion."

The Groton parson was very likely more scrupulous in his attitude toward the Indians than were the powerful negotiators for their lands, and he may have been morally correct in opposing the scheme of cession. But diplomatically he was impossible. At once he aroused the hot enmity of Sir William, and he managed to make a bad matter worse by revealing the fact that Wheelock was himself after a land grant. That was an irretrievable blunder. When the dire tidings of its making reached Wheelock by special messenger, he at once despatched another friend, Reverend Ebenezer

Cleaveland, to see if the damage could not be undone. This gentleman found himself powerless, but he saw the end of the council. It came on a Saturday, and that night Sir William and his family prudently departed and advised all the other palefaces to do likewise. He knew what was about to happen.

The good Mr. Cleaveland remained overnight, believing that Sunday would at least be fairly tranquil. But he counted without the firewater. "Within two hours after the rum had been given out", he reported, "the whole street and parade was filled with drunkenness, and nothing could be heard or seen but yelling and fighting, as though hell itself had broke loose." Four had been slain in the orgies before Cleaveland fled the spot at ten the next morning. The result of this deliberate debauchery of the Indians was a new strip of land, eight hundred miles long and one hundred wide, for the English.

But this fiasco helped to hasten the locating and the founding of Dartmouth College. Schoolmaster Eleazar now knew that his eye was cast upon the Mohawk country vainly. Even the region of the Susquehanna, long favored by him, was not obtainable under conditions that suited. Where to go, then? for going he had determined upon, as well as to pay more attention to the educating of white pupils. He must have English blood in better proportion for his work.

Offers of locations for the Charity School had been and still were plentiful. Dozens of towns and small settlements from the Kennebec to the " Father of Waters " applied for the honor of becoming the seat of the future Dartmouth College. Reverend Charles J. Smith had devised a scheme for its settlement in Virginia or Carolina. People in the vicinity of Albany offered a location only to have it declined on the ground that " the religious character of Albany is such that it would by no means do to take the school into it ", whereat the good burghers of that town were somewhat disconcerted, and " took your reflections upon their city a little in dudgeon." Captain A. J. Lansing offered money and land at Lansingburg in New York. Some Philadelphia Presbyterians proposed a gift of territory not far from Pittsburgh; Stockbridge, in Massachusetts, became a candidate for the location; so did Pittsfield, upon which it was reported to Wheelock: " the commissioners in Boston oppose the school, and will do so if it be placed in New Hampshire, if they think it vies with Cambridge. But the greatest part of the people want another College as a check upon the extravagant demands made there." The suggestion was made by New York patrons of the school that it be made " an annexation to the College of New Jersey." This met short shrift with Wheelock, who had no notion of letting anybody but the Almighty have any division of authority with himself.

In all this period of sifting, selecting, and then rejecting, New Hampshire had ever stood as a sort of promised land if others failed. As far back as 1765, Governor Benning Wentworth of that province had promised five hundred acres of land " to encourage the school." His son, the brilliant, debonair, luxury-loving, yet sensible and honorable Governor John Wentworth, was as well inclined, and in March, 1768, wrote Wheelock: " I shall be ready to grant a township on Connecticut River of six miles square for an endowment of the school."

This real promise of substantial help; the fact that many of Wheelock's Connecticut friends and neighbors had gone north and settled along the river; the belief that the Canadian Indians could be induced to attend a school located in New Hampshire, and above all the strong probability of being able to obtain a charter decided Wheelock to pull up the Indian Charity School by the roots and transplant it to the new lands far up the east bank of the Connecticut River. The English trustees were agreeable to the change; Wheelock set about the framing of a charter which he sent to Governor Wentworth August 22, 1769. In it he termed the new institution an academy, but added as a postscript this historic suggestion:

"Sir — if proper to use the word 'College' instead of 'Academy' in the charter I shall be well pleased with it."

That postscript was the real founding of Dartmouth College.

The completed charter was delivered into the hands of its first president in March, 1770. It used the name "College" as he had wished and named the institution for Lord Dartmouth, after Governor Wentworth had modestly put the honor by. But the English trustees, including Dartmouth himself, were wrathful over the rather subtle evolution of the Indian Charity School into Dartmouth College. Even the good-natured Thornton wrote: "I am afraid there is too much worldly wisdom in this charter, and that it is trusting man instead of resting on the living God." It is probable that the unexpectedness of the move shocked the Englishmen more than any imagined evil in it; truth to tell, Wheelock had kept his trustees entirely in the dark as to the charter until it was obtained. Their charge of disingenuousness against him was deserved. Still they doled out money to him as an individual — they never officially recognized him as President of Dartmouth College — until the fund was exhausted.

That the idea of Indian education was still strong with Wheelock and his friends is made clear by the phrasing of the charter. Said Governor Wentworth in the name of George III:

We do of our special grace, certain knowledge and mere motion, ordain, grant & constitute that there be a college erected in our said province of New Hampshire by the name of Dartmouth College for the education & instruction of Youth of the Indian Tribes in this Land in reading, writing & all parts of Learning which shall appear necessary and expedient for civilizing & christianizing Children of Pagans as well as in all liberal Arts and Sciences; and also of English Youth and any others, . . . and not excluding any Person of any religious denomination whatsoever from free & equal liberty & advantage of Education or from any of the liberties and privileges or immunities of the said College on account of his or their speculative sentiments in Religion, & of his or their being of a religious profession different from the said Trustees of the said Dartmouth College.

Even with the charter safely signed, sealed, and delivered, Eleazar Wheelock's troubles were not ended. Immediately there arose such a clamor from New Hampshire towns eager to possess the college that one would have thought the chief end and aim of each of them was to be the seat of an institution of learning.

Wheelock made an eight weeks' tour of the north country in the spring of 1770, and when the wrangling and backbiting were over, chose Hanover as the home for his college; the site was the finest and most advantageous in his eyes, and the town was " settled with the most serious, steady inhabitants." They have left many descendants.

Thereupon arose an almost incredible bedlam of protest from some of the disappointed places. Wheelock was jeered at as a visionary, called a double-dealer, and even accused of some sort of underhand scheme to feather the nest of himself and his family by the settling in Hanover. Even his friend Colonel Jonathan Moulton wrote to him from Orford:

I have been in Portsmouth, and there to hear all mouths opened against you, and laughing at me and all my neighborhood, flinging, " Ah! I always told you Dr. Wheelock was making a purse to himself; and now this of fixing the College proves it." Your usefulness at present in the dear Redeemer's kingdom seems over. Oh, sir! consider, this affair seems to overthrow in the minds of sinners all you have been building up so many years, and it is currently talked that those that have largely subscribed will not pay one farthing, except forced, if the College stands in Hanover; and others say it can't prosper, for it's all a jockey trick from first to last.

Wheelock stood up to the blast unmoved, like the strong man that he was. "The site for Dartmouth College", he replied, "was not determined by any private interest or party on earth, but the Redeemer's."

The first president of Dartmouth was, it is evident, firmly of the opinion that the Almighty and himself were on terms that admitted of no disruption by any terrestrial powers.

CHAPTER III

THERE are those who from time to time and for reasons peculiar to themselves venture to question the entire appropriateness of many of the mottoes that adorn college seals. " Truth " and " Light " and " Onward " and " Upward " and the whole tribe of self-congratulatory parts of speech have had their doubters here and there. But of Dartmouth it may confidently be asserted that the " Vox Clamantis in Deserto " was absolutely and indisputably fitting when it was engraved upon her Great Seal.

The wilderness where her voice was raised was pervasive, insistent, omnipresent. Some ultra-urban young gentlemen, it is occasionally whispered, profess to find like conditions to this very day when they first arrive in Hanover, but they generally develop into the most ardent champions of the great out-of-doors the college can boast.

However, there was no quibbling as to nature's primitive garb when in early August, 1770, Eleazar Wheelock, with his ox-teams and his laborers and

The Old Bridge

two companions, Sylvanus Ripley and John Crane, pushed his straggling and struggling way up from Connecticut and at last reached the grant which was to be the home of the Indian Charity School and Dartmouth College. To the westward flowed the Connecticut, that beautiful boulevard for Indian travel from north to south, and upon the sparkling waters of which the redskin's canoe was still occasionally to be seen, but which was as yet uncurbed by dams and uncrossed by bridges. To the east were rugged, densely wooded hills, presently to rise into bare and towering mountains.

On the level plateau selected as the location for the college, giant pines nearing three hundred feet in height shut out the very sun, save at noon, and calmed the fiercest blasts of the upper air into a cathedral quietude. To the north it was two miles to the nearest human habitation "through one continued and dreary wood." The bear, the wolf, the lynx, and the panther roamed the forest and doubtless scented the approach of President Wheelock's domestic animals with an instinct toward making trouble for them, which they afterwards did. The good doctor had desired a place for his college "remote from the allurements of more populous towns." He had surely found it.

A few axemen had preceded the Wheelock party

and had carved a small resting-place from the prodigious pines. Soon after the president's arrival, a log house, eighteen feet square, with windows of mica and oiled paper, was erected for his use. This was "the first sprout of the college", and around it later were built huts for the student dormitories. That that first dwelling was highly honored by Wheelock was made evident by the inclusion of it in his will as a bequest to his son and successor. It long since vanished into the limbo of regretted things, torn down in 1783 to feed the flames of some unappreciative student revel.

Mahomet had gone to the mountain, and now Mahomet's students must come to Mahomet. Wheelock, whose comparison with the prophet is not altogether forced, found his "primitive Alcazar" in a few weeks ready for the translation of his pupils of the Indian Charity School from Lebanon to the wilds of Hanover. Madame Wheelock and the family were also to come, together with four slaves, Exeter, Brister, Chloe, and Peggy. The independent ways of these bondsmen at that time appear from the report of Wheelock's nephew and chief teamster, Jabez Bingham, who wrote from Connecticut that "Exeter is very high in the instep, and says he won't go without Peggy goes and all his things."

34

Wheelock had arranged with his wife that she was to start in mid-September; on the tenth he wrote her some final instructions, quaint, religious and practical at once. " I hope I am in God's way ", he said, and then: " It will not be best for Brister to bring his cow unless she gives milk; it will cost 40s. at least to winter her here. Let some factor buy 100 lb. or more of tobacco and bring . . . If you have a barrel of Old Pork, bring it with you. . . . You would do well to bring a gross of pipes." Bingham reported to his uncle before the start from Lebanon that " Sir Cluet has got a barrel of rum and a barrel of molasses, a cag of wine and half a barrel of Shuggar ", and that the articles would be brought up.

The president found soon after his letter of the tenth that failure to discover water near his newly built house necessitated its removal, with the consequent delaying of even a shelter over the heads of Madame Wheelock and the students. He made strenuous efforts to prevent the departure from Lebanon, sending Doctor Crane as a special messenger, with license, so far as he was concerned, to travel on Sunday. This was Crane's credential:

This may certify that the urgency and importance of the journey of Dr. Crane the Bearer is such as that I suppose will be tho suff to justify his riding upon the

Sabbath in order to accomplish the Design on which he is sent, which is to prevent my family & the members of Dartmouth College setting out from Lebanon on Tuesday next according to appointment, which by reason of some unforeseen providences will be earlier than provision can be made for their reception, — the occasion & circumstances of which the Doctor is able to relate, and therefore his encouragement and countenance in his journey is humbly requested of all concerned by their humble servt.

Wheelock was not above compromising with the powers of darkness when it seemed best to him.

Doctor Crane rode gallantly and well down the rough valley, and he met the northern bound procession indeed, but too late to turn it back. Madame Wheelock, from the rocking depths of her great English coach, a gift from John Thornton, declared that having begun the journey, *dux femina facti*, she would carry it through. Doctor Crane could do nothing but turn himself about and join the strange procession.

Strange it surely was. A horseman or two at the head; Madame Wheelock's splendid coach, long the marvel of the countryside, drawn by disgruntled and panting steeds; the ox-teams, bearing the justly celebrated barrel of rum and the other lesser appurtenances of life; the negro servitors and the cow, and the thirty students, of whom but two

were Indians, tramping along on foot — never was
there a more remarkable pilgrimage for the intellectual than these elements presented. Pushing
forward a few miles a day; at the last part of the
journey toiling up the fearfully rough " Great
Road " skirting the Connecticut River; staggering,
lurching, jouncing over the scarcely opened way,
the cavalcade reached the college clearing only to
find everything in dire confusion.

Wheelock, who saw the hand of the Lord in most
exigencies, was undismayed. He housed his stuff
with his wife " and the females of my family " in
the original log hut, and compelled his sons and
students to make booths and beds of hemlock
boughs — the woodcraft of the two Indians doubtless being of much assistance in this work of establishing Dartmouth's first dormitories.

Tutor Woodward, arriving from Boston at this
juncture, with a few more students, vividly describes the state of things at the clearing. " It was
near the close of the day," he says: " there was
scanty room in the Doctor's shanty for the shelter
of those who were on the ground, and none for us
who had just arrived. All constructed for a temporary residence a tent of crotched stakes and poles
covered with boughs. It was soon ready, and we
camped down wrapped in our blankets, and for a

time slept very comfortably. During the night, however, a storm arose of high wind and pelting rain. Our tent came down and buried us in its ruins. After mutual inquiry, we found no one injured, and as the storm raged without abated fury, we resolved to abide the issue as we were, and wait for the day. When fair weather returned, we made more substantial booths for our protection till better accommodations could be provided."

These conditions were soon improved. A house of timber and boards, brought from sawmills some miles away, was built for the president. It was forty by thirty-two feet and one story high, with a little attic for the doctor's office, while the servants were given a better dwelling eighty by thirty-two and two stories high. Wheelock assumed no airs of greatness. Huts for the students were hastily constructed, and, with his brood around him, Eleazar Wheelock set his institution in order for the facing of its first winter.

Snow came heavily down upon the " groves of the academy ", as a later president was fond of saying, before the roof of the new college building was laid on. There was no chapel. " Sometimes," wrote David McClure, one of the faculty, " Dr. Wheelock presented to God their morning and evening prayers standing at the head of his numer-

ous family in the *open air;* and the surrounding
forest for the first time reverberated the solemn
sounds of supplication and praise." Surely a scene
for the historical painter who will some day arise
with the love of the ancient Dartmouth in his heart
and the genius for a noble picture in his brush. For
his title he will need but borrow from the Great
Seal: " Vox Clamantis in Deserto."

CHAPTER IV

GETTING UNDER WAY

EARLY in 1770 the main building, the " college ", was completed. Its unreadiness in the
autumn before, together with an actual scarcity of
food, had been the cause of the return of a number
of the pupils to Connecticut for the winter. Eat-
ables were costly for those days, owing to the im-
mense labor of hauling and the difficulty in raising
crops. Beef was at twenty shillings a hundred and
pork at thirty-three. Wheat cost six shillings a
bushel; rye, three shillings, sixpence, and Indian
corn two shillings, sixpence; molasses brought five
shillings a gallon.

As the tuition and board of a student was but
twenty pounds a year, Dartmouth's profits were
slim enough, if the students were to get anything to
eat. The greater part of their provender had to be
transported more than a hundred miles through
new and bad roads. Some of it came up the Connecticut in bateaux, in which case it was necessary
to carry the stuff around a dozen falls or rapids. If

there was a lack of luxuries, the savagery of nature was mostly at fault.

But the new building was something of a triumph under the circumstances. It was two stories in height and twice as long as any of the other structures. Sixteen rooms, besides kitchen, hall, and storeroom, furnished the students with commons and dormitories. There was a smaller "school house", presumably for recitations. Soon a barn, a wash-house, and a bakehouse were added to the outfit. The president's new frame dwelling was found, "through God's favor", to be fairly comfortable. By the summer of 1771 a good deal of land had been cleared, and the college seat took on the airs and appearance of a village.

Dartmouth's first commencement was a great event for the wilderness. Riding up from Portsmouth on horseback came Governor Wentworth with a company of sixty gentlemen from Portsmouth, making camp two nights on the way. With them came the glorious silver punch-bowl that is still one of the cherished possessions of the college, though the years of disuse have long since obliterated the faintest odor of the New England rum that was wont to waft good cheer from its capacious interior. Four students took their degrees as bachelors of arts: Levi Frisbie, Sylvanus Ripley,

Samuel Gray, and John Wheelock, all of whom had emigrated from their Yale classes to graduate at Dartmouth. The exercises, which took place on August 28, were as follows:

1. A Salutatory Oration in English, by Ripley, upon the Virtues, succeeded by an Anthem.

2. A Clyosophic Oration in Latin, by Frisbie.

3. A Syllogistic Disputation, wherein Gray held the question, *An vera cognitio Dei Luce Naturae acquiri potest?* Opposed by Frisbie, Wheelock, and Ripley; and

4. A Valedictory Oration in Latin, by Wheelock, " followed by an anthem composed and set to music by the young gentlemen, candidates for a degree."

This appeal to the Muses must have been a moving performance. Wheelock says that Ripley's oration " produced tears from a great number of the learned ", and this, too, before the punch was ladled from the silver bowl. Frisbie recited an original poem, with these concluding lines:

" Thus Dartmouth, happy in her sylvan seat,
Drinks the pure pleasures of her fair retreat,
Her songs of praise in notes melodious rise
Like clouds of incense to the skies.
Her God protects her with paternal care
From ills destructive and each fatal snare;
And may He still protect, and she adore,
Till heaven, and earth, and time shall be no more."

GETTING UNDER WAY

Semi-official history says that the various orations, disputations, and the poem were delivered *al fresco*, a crude stage of logs and hewn boards, to which access was given by a broad, inclined hemlock plank, furnishing the rostrum for the four who were forever to hold their conspicuous place in Dartmouth annals. There is a tradition, characteristic enough to be true, that an Indian under-classman had some share in the public exercises, and that he refused to have anything to do with the platform but spoke his piece in aboriginal tongue, from the huge branch of an adjacent pine. However that may be, there is no gloomy cloud of scepticism over the statement that Governor Wentworth paid for the ox that was barbecued on the green, nor that a barrel of rum was broached, to the great satisfaction of the settlers for miles around.

But to the president, this first Commencement was not an unalloyed joy. Madame Wheelock was too ill to receive any guests, and the presidential cook, with the almost inevitable instinct of that profession, seized upon the occasion to get drunk. But Eleazar Wheelock was ever of undaunted soul, and he invited the dashing governor and his merry suite to dinner, some of which he perhaps prepared with his own hands. Under the circumstances it could hardly have been a luxurious feast, yet some of the Portsmouth visitors were of mean and little souls enough to sneer at the bareness of their entertainment after they had returned home.

Wheelock's answer, resembling somewhat Johnson's famous letter to Chesterfield in its simplicity, its dignity, and its touch of pathos, must have made those snobbish critics ashamed of themselves. " We were indeed", he said, "in very trying circumstances; but we got along as well as we could, depending on the candor and clemency of our friends. As to the table-linen, which I hear is complained of, that must come, I suspect, wholly upon me, through my poverty. My expenses having been so long inadequate to my means, I had provided no better, though I did not know till then that their want was so great as not to be able to appear decent in home-made, till the Commencement was over. As to the College, it owns but one [tablecloth], that was lately given by a generous lady in Connecticut, and of her own manufacture. But we are getting along, and things are growing better."

We may feel sure that Governor Wentworth had no part in the petty fault-finding. He honored and assisted Wheelock in every way possible until the approaching storm of the Revolution swept him out of the country. He attended two more Commencements, and he put through the building of a new road from his summer seat at Wolfeboro to Hanover — a terrible affair across the shoulder of Moose Mountain and long since given over to the newer forest, the plough, and the stone-heap. If Yale gave much to Dartmouth in the person of Wheelock and the first graduating class, Harvard's gift of the brilliant, well educated cavalier who was the college's best friend in the days of its dawning, was hardly less valuable.

The first college year ended so auspiciously that the president felt justified in sending forth a prospectus in which he declared that: "The Rev. Dr. Wheelock, through the surprising smiles of Heaven upon his unwearied endeavors, has now so nearly effected his great and arduous undertaking to settle and accommodate his Indian school and college in a howling wilderness that he has the fairest prospect in a little time to be able to support an hundred Indian and English youths upon charity, and all with a view to the first and grand object of the Institution, viz., the spreading the blessed gospel of the Redeemer among the savages."

Poverty's white horse rode o' nights in the Hanover forests, however, and must have caused the resolute Wheelock many waking hours. The Indian Charity School fund in England was becoming exhausted, with no hope of renewal. The Scotch board in Edinburgh was so angry at the development that it expressed " apprehensions that Dartmouth College will contribute little to the conversion of the heathen, and after the Doctor's death fall into Episcopal management " — this a rap at Governor Wentworth, the Church of England man, and some of the trustees. Only a few driblets of money were forthcoming from that strait-laced and suspicious quarter.

" My necessities really call for help," wrote Wheelock to John Thornton, May, 1773. Of course there was the Provincial Assembly to look to for aid, as in the cases of so many other ante-Revolution colleges. But the New Hampshire Assembly was not easily aroused to enthusiasm for Dartmouth. The quarrel over the location still rankled, and even Governor Wentworth's repeated recommendations were coldly received. In March, 1771, the Assembly had voted the munificent sum of sixty pounds for Wheelock " in consideration of his great services for the interest of said College." Good John Phillips, of Exeter, did much better than that with gifts of £175 and £125. In June, 1771, the Assembly was stormed by a couple of student lobbyists, John Wheelock and Sylvanus Ripley, but in vain. The trustees' prayer that a salary be granted President Wheelock from the Provincial treasury was expeditiously tabled. Even the president's own appeal for the right to set up a lottery to raise five thousand pounds for the erection of the proposed "large house" was denied, though probably not from any squeamishness at the notion of a learned doctor of divinity promoting a gambling affair.

But willing to do something if it cost no money, the Assembly fished for Lord Dartmouth's aid when he was appointed Secretary of State for the Colonies, imploring "your Lordship's patronage for the good people we represent, and especially for our established seminary of literature, to which we hope, if your Lordship be a nursing father, it will be a diffusive blessing and thereby merit in some measure the exalted name of Dartmouth College." In May, 1773, the Assembly did pass a grant of five hundred pounds to help erect the new college building. Thus the sum of £560 was the limit of the Provincial Assembly's aid to Dartmouth. Subsequently Wheelock trained his guns on the Continental Congress, and through the powerful favor of Patrick Henry, Chairman of the Committee on Indian Affairs, obtained a grant of five hundred dollars.

A subscription was ordered by the trustees in the spring of 1775, and it gave every appearance of being a great success, as between four and five thousand pounds were promised. But not a dollar was ever collected; the onset of the war gave the subscribers other things to think of in connection with their money than the necessities of a struggling college and Indian school far in the north wilderness. So the College Hall remained for many years the remodeled and enlarged first Wheelock house (after the log hut), to which thirty feet and a belfry had been added. This structure was innocent of paint, inside and out, and the platform of the " great room ", used as chapel, meeting-house and public hall, was built of axe-hewn planks. The building stood near the old well, from which the college pump supplied long generations of students with water even up to modern times. The first College Hall was in the southeast corner of what is now the campus and close to the site of the present Reed Hall.

By Commencement, 1774, the college was well under way. Its general appearance was accurately described by Doctor Jeremy Belknap, that famous theological tilter, who rode up from Dover on horseback to witness the exercises. In his diary he wrote:

" After dinner walked down to the Connecticut River opposite to the College, where is a ferry. Observed on a tree, where the bark was cut off, the figure of an Indian painted, which was done by one of the Indian scholars. At evening prayers, by the President's desire, I preached a sermon in the College hall. Supped and lodged at the President's. In the evening the front of the College was illuminated.

" The plain where the College stands is large and pleasant, and the land good. The College is about seventy or eighty feet long and thirty broad, containing twenty chambers. The hall is a distinct building, which also serves for a meeting-house, and the kitchen is in one end of it. The President's house stands on a rising ground east of the College, and to the north of this is the place proposed to build the new college, near a quarry of gray stone which is intended for the material of the building. There is another quarry, much larger, about three quarters of a mile distant. The tutors are Messrs. Woodward, Ripley, Wheelock, and Smith; the two former are married to the President's daughters. Several tradesmen and taverners are settled round the College in good buildings, — which gives the place the appearance of a village. . . . It is really surprising to observe the improvements that have been made in few years. . . ."

With progress came — early, in Dartmouth's case — the inevitable revolt that every college faces at some time in its career: the uproar over poor provisions for the appetite and stomach in Commons. The trouble was started by some young gentlemen students from Portsmouth, to whom Eleazar Wheelock's backwoods fare did not appeal after their luxurious home tables. They wrote hot letters of protest to their parents and even sent by special messenger some samples of a particularly repulsive bread as evidence of the justice of their protests. The president, returning from a trip to the down-country in a towering rage, expelled the ringleader in the uprising and indefinitely suspended several others. But, though he could play the imperator at Hanover, he could not suppress the scandal, which had gotten far beyond his precincts. Even the genial and always friendly Governor Wentworth was stirred to action. Under date of July 6, 1774, he wrote to Wheelock:

MY DEAR AND REVEREND FRIEND, — Amidst the variety of important and naturally perplexing affairs which deeply engage my mind at this very disquieted juncture of American agitations, nothing lies nearer my heart than the interest and honor of Dartmouth College, with which yours is inseparably connected. It is therefore with the utmost grief that I perform the strict duty of friendship to both in telling you that it is reported and rapidly gains belief that your provision for the students is extremely bad, their entertainment neither clean, plentiful, nor wholesome, though the price and expense exceeds for comfortable living; that the youth are thereby unhealthy and debilitated, their constitutions impaired, and their friends and parents highly disgusted. These reports assail me on all sides from those who have and those who have not children under your care. . . .

Wholesome, sound, and plentiful food must be provided. The very name of putrefied, stinking provisions in a College alarms parents, who wish to secure health to their sons. Twenty oxen badly saved had better be cast into the river and perish, than one month's improper diet be given to the students. I would not wish to see profusion or delicacy enter our walls. Cleanliness, plenty, and plainness should never be absent.

Belknap evidently found the uprising in full swing on his Commencement visit to Dartmouth. "The President," says his diary, "appears to be much affected with the reports that are circulated concerning the badness of the provisions, on which account some have left the College. Last evening he entered into a large and warm vindication of himself, declaring that the reports are all false, and that he did not doubt but 'God would bring forth his righteousness as the light, and his judgment as the noonday.' He has had the mortification to lose two cows, and the rest were greatly hurt by a contagious distemper, so that they could not have a full supply of milk; and once that the pickle leaked out of the beef barrel, so that the meat was not so sweet. He had been ill-used with respect to the purchase of some wheat, so that they had smutty bread for a while. The scholars, on the other hand, say they scarce ever had anything but pork and greens, without vinegar, and pork and potatoes, that fresh meat comes but very seldom, and that the victuals are very badly dressed."

To this the paying students (the charity pupils having been shown the wisdom of signing a paper declaring that the bad food stories were " false and abusive ") added that their Commons breakfast was " mostly the leaves of wintergreen made into a tea, and even that often sweetened with molasses; many times only broth for breakfast, then coffee or chocolate, usually sweetened with molasses, and beef unfit to eat."

The trustees finally felt compelled to take cognizance of the outcry. They investigated and resolved that the complaints were groundless, " only that for a few days some beef was served by the cook which (though accidentally tainted in a small degree) was judged by them to be such as the students will generally approve."

Wheelock's cooks, it may be said, were the bane of his life, what with their affiliation with New England rum and their unclassical lack of the proper distinction between *meum* and *tuum*. On one occasion a couple were ordered to the whipping-post together for their thievery.

But the cooks were not altogether responsible for the protests against the college provender that came to the surface periodically for years, under the régimes of all sorts of stewards, agents, purveyors, or whatever their titles may have been. Chase records that in the reign of one Roger Sargent, " at one time, the butter being persistently strong, one of the students (afterwards a distinguished lawyer of New Hampshire) was deputed, while all the others stood at their places, to apostrophize the offensive stuff and bid it ' down ' from their sight. It is said that the rebuke was effectual."

Another of Wheelock's troubles were the tavern-keepers in the settlement and across the Connecticut River. In spite of the president's protest and even Governor Wentworth's influence, they received licenses from the court to sell liquor. Payne's inn, near the college, which seems to have been the most disreputable of all, obtained its permit by reason of the pique of one Sympson, the high sheriff, who thought he had been slighted at the first Commencement. Payne did not hesitate to supply the students with rum, and, though a stern edict against visiting taverns had been issued in the second year, the place was much frequented.

Even Wheelock's sons were occasional sinners in this regard.

The *Dartmouth* of July, 1843, printed a reminiscence of Reverend Noah Miles, a student in the first Wheelock's time, on this subject: "It seems that Mr. Miles's chum, having indulged in a spree at Payne's tavern, came home very drunk and sick. He was sent for to the President's study, but being too sick to go, Miles went in his stead, rapped, and entered. The President was busy at his writing-table, with his great white wig on his head. The conversation was something like this: 'Ah, Miles! it is you. But where is your chum? I sent for him; why does he not come?' 'Sir, he is not able to come.' 'But he can walk, can he not?' 'Sir, he cannot stand upon his feet.' 'Indeed, then he is badly done up. This is a miserable affair. That tavern is a nuisance. But can you tell me, Miles, whether my sons Eleazar and James were there?' 'Sir, I understand that they were.' 'Ah! I suspected it. Bad boys of mine! I have some hopes of James yet; but as to Eleazar he will be damned, I believe.' "

Wheelock thundered against the nuisance even in the pulpit. Payne responded by tearing down the president's fence under some pretext or other and with authority as highway surveyor. Then one Joseph Skinner, " not knowing the fear of God before his eyes and being moved by the instigation of the Devil ", tacked up on the door of the College Hall a writing calling the president a liar and a hypocrite who was bound for hell. For this pleasantry he had to pay twenty shillings and costs. Some sophomores and freshmen petitioned that they might use some of their spare time " in stepping the minuet and learning the sword." Such were a few of the crosses of the founder. Yet he had some consolation. In February, 1775, he wrote of a great religious revival:

Love, peace, and joy reign triumphant. The only discourse now in fashion when students visit at one another's rooms is of the things of the Kingdom of Heaven. And it would be a reproach to anyone if he should introduce anything frothy, vain, trifling, or unprofitable into conversation. . . . It has seemed to be wholly confined to the College, until within a few days it has spread to all the houses in the neighborhood, excepting one, viz., a tavern [Payne's]; and my little captive boys discover that something uncommon is the matter, and are often in tears.

But Dartmouth grew in spite of, perhaps because of, its trials and difficulties. In March, 1772, it housed fifty students, including six Indians; in November, 1774, there were a hundred, of whom twenty-one were Indians. The reputation of the college spread abroad. In 1775 Reverend Joseph Huntington wrote that in Connecticut it " was generally esteemed the best on the continent." Very likely Wheelock's statement that he thought it proper " to let the world know that there is no encouragement given that such as are vain, idle, trifling, flesh-pleasing . . . will be admitted here " had something to do with enhancing admiration for the college among the Connecticut godly.

By the beginning of the Revolution, the Indian problem became serious. Some good redskins had come to Hanover, among them sons of the St. Francis chiefs to the north. In fact, Canada had now become the recruiting ground for Wheelock, who maintained as late as in 1773 that " the Indians are the first object in the charter." Ten came from the Caghenanagas in 1772. A few Hurons were obtained. But it was evident from the moment of the trouble on Lexington Green that the supply of aborigines for Dartmouth was to cease. The Canadian Indians were restless ever and not so amenable to restraint as their brothers of the New England and New York provinces had been. The white students disliked and mistrusted them and complained of their perpetual " hollowing and making all manner of noise." They had a penchant for " big beer ", as they called it, even the youngsters.

Had there been no Revolution, it was still inevitable that the Indians would have been lost to Dartmouth, retreating into the forests before the white man's overwhelming civilization and refusing to come out. The Indian Charity School could never again have been pulled up to follow them. Wheelock's intentions remained honest to the last, but circumstances were stronger than his will, of iron though it was.

Dartmouth's career during the Revolutionary War was peaceful enough, compared with the troubles of other American colleges. Her isolation was an advantage, though rendering her open to Indian attacks, which, however, came no nearer than Royalton in Vermont. Undoubtedly her peculiar relations to the red tribes counted much in her favor. As to the war itself, no military operations reached anywhere near the college, though Lord Dartmouth was anxious enough to entreat " that the safety of the College might be recommended to both General Sir William Howe and his brother the Admiral ", thus revealing an impression on the noble earl's part that the Connecticut could be ascended by a fleet of war-ships.

But if not visible, warfare was audible, for it has always been asserted that the booming of the guns of Bunker Hill was heard in Hanover. The president's diary contains this: " June 16 — The noise of cannon supposed to be at Boston, was heard all day. 17th — The same reports of cannon. We wait with impatience to hear the occasion and the event." The noise was first noted by Daniel Simons, an Indian sophomore, who happened to be lying with his ear to the ground. Hard to believe as the story is, the diary, the noises, and the dates would seem to establish its accuracy.

It is proudly held by local historians that there never was a Tory in Hanover after Concord and Lexington. Certainly, if any one there had justification for leaning toward the royalists, it was the president of Dartmouth College. His funds had mostly come from England and were now to be shut off. His location and many favors of all kinds were from the powerful hand and the kindly heart of the royal governor, John Wentworth. His outlook, with these sources of assistance gone, was gloomy enough. But when once the irrepressible conflict was seen to be preparing, he did not waive his allegiance to liberty. As early as November, 1774, he dared write to Wentworth of " the cause of liberty which is so justly dear to them " (Bostonians) and in April, 1775, to Thornton, the Englishman:

" I believe there never was a more dutiful, loyal, and well-affected people to Government than has ever been in these colonies till the Stamp Act. And the colonies have ever been propense to peace and reconciliation till those horrid murders and savage butcheries, so inhumanly committed under pretence of reducing rebels to obedience. The wringing of the nose bringeth forth blood. Our liberties were dearly bought, and we have tasted the sweetness of them, and esteem them our birthright; and perhaps his Majesty will find they will not be given up so tamely as he imagines. The colonies seem to be determined they will not be slaves."

The British friends of the college were tremendously enraged at this, but the patriotism of Eleazar Wheelock had been proven, to his eternal glory. He had the satisfaction of seeing no Commencement, nor scarcely any regular exercise of the college omitted during the war, so long as he lived. Nor was there any interruption after his death.

Wheelock's son John was a lieutenant-colonel in Bedel's regiment and did good service against Brant's Indians in New York, where one of his father's former pupils, Butler, was committing many atrocities against the whites. He afterward was on General Gates' staff with the same rank. James and Eleazar also saw military service of one sort and another, the latter arousing the anger of his sire by enlisting one Denning, " a laborer which I most depended on, and I think it a flagrant evidence of want of duty, affection and tenderness in my son toward an aged and afflicted father, on the verge of the grave and oppressed with a weight of cares enough for an angel." The elder Eleazar was no doting parent.

At the time of that writing in his diary, the president was, indeed, nearing the Angel of the End, and he knew it. For some years he had been tormented by asthma and a persistent skin ailment. In the first month of 1779 epileptic seizures began to rack his frame. Pathetically he wrote to Nathaniel Whitaker: " I now feel more than ever the want of a pension, which I think the world owes me, with which I might buy a cask of wine and other suitable spirits which my physicians all advise to be necessary for me, also coffee, chocolate, tea, etc., which I am obliged to live wholly without for want of money to purchase the same."

But outwardly Wheelock fought death as he had fought nature, and obstacles, and men; slanders, politics, and hostile intrigues. He could no more have laid down life and its all-possessing interests without a struggle, pious fatalist though he was, than he could tamely submit to the charge of being a Tory because he chanced to celebrate Thanksgiving at Dartmouth on the wrong date through a perfectly pardonable error. He taught and preached till he had to be carried to the hall in a chair, and then, too weak for that, received the students in his own house. He died almost standing, for on the last day it is told of him that "he walked the room without assistance and talked with composure." "O my family, be faithful unto death" was his final, and, in the light of the after years, strangely significant utterance. On the day of his passing, April 24, 1779, he was a few days less than sixty-eight years of age.

Thus went to his fathers a man around the estimate of whose qualities there has long been and perhaps will always be a conflict of opinion. It is clear that those who liked him could never be shaken in their loyalty, and that those who disliked him did so with a cordiality usually reserved for the devil in that era, which proves his individuality and strength of character. We know his tenacity of purpose and his unfailing courage. That he was quarrelsome and vain and given to assuming too much of a monopoly in the knowledge of the plans of Providence may be more than suspected. But his littlenesses were very little and his greatness very great indeed.

Eleazar was a supreme dictator in the college he had made, but to be just that was a necessity under the circumstances. He was patriarchal in his ways, and there must have been a gentler side to his nature that history rather loses sight of, for many of his students have written of him with genuine affection. On the simple slab that covers his tomb in the lovely cemetery at Hanover, where trees and grasses and mossy glens form a perfect picture of peace, is inscribed this epitaph to a man of action:

" By the Gospel he subdued the ferocity of the savage;
And to the civilized he opened new paths of science.
Traveller,
Go, if you can, and deserve
The sublime reward of such merit."

That challenge, which in effect bids the traveler fare forth and create another Dartmouth College, if he is able, might have come from the very lips of him of the lion heart who lies under it.

CHAPTER V

THE REIGN OF THE CROWN PRINCE

WHEN John, the Crown Prince of the dynasty of Wheelock, received word of his accession to the rule of Dartmouth College, he was in New Jersey with General Gates. Bezaleel Woodward, Eleazar's son-in-law and the ranking member of the faculty, acted as president in the brief interval before the soldier should return. Woodward was a man of great ability, an astute politician and a skilful contender. He might have made a better president than did Prince John, had his selection been possible, yet the very failings of the founder's son produced a condition that did more for Dartmouth and every other college in the country than any successful administration could possibly have accomplished.

But the charter had given Eleazar Wheelock the power to name his successor, and in his will he declared: " I do therefore hereby nominate, constitute, and appoint my said son, JOHN WHEELOCK, to be my successor in said office of President of my Indian Charity School, and Dartmouth College, with and into which said School is now incorporated. And to him I give and grant all my right, title, and claim to said seminary, and all the appurtenances, interest, jurisdiction, power, and authority to, in, and over the same belonging to me, as the founder of it, or by grant in the charter to me, or by any other ways or means whatsoever."

The colonel, who reached Hanover for the August Commencement, was a bit inclined to shy at the difficult task. The college was like a ship without a rudder, now that the elder Wheelock had gone and with him the one-man paternalism that was the very essence of the institution. The finances were in sorry shape; it was estimated by Colonel Elisha Payne, the treasurer, that if all the corporate property were sold at public vendue, the proceeds would not pay the college's debts. Receipts from students were less than eighty pounds a year. The buildings were constantly growing more shabby and some were dry-rotting.

To add to the general gloom, the war had depleted the supply of students until there were now only about thirty altogether, although the " School ", the preparatory department, was well attended. Even food was scarce, owing to crop failures and the falling purchasing power of Continental money. Sylvanus Ripley believed " that the College would have been broken for want of provisions, if it had not been for the resolute exertions of Professor Woodward." The trustees, however, seem to have felt no particular alarm, for they permitted the college to pay three hundred pounds (currency at twenty to one) for their delectation at Commencement, bills for spirituous comforts having no small share in the expenditures.

Another thing that had torn and harassed the college, made powerful enemies for it, and hurt its usefulness was the bitter political fight that had been raging for some years between New Hampshire and New York for the possession of Vermont and the strip east of the Connecticut River. Hanover had become the storm-center of the battle, and the " College Party " most active in the affair.

The Dartmouth part of the town now set up a separate organization, calling itself Dresden. A printing-press was hurried up from Connecticut at the elder Wheelock's request, and a paper called the *Mercury* established on the college plain, from which vitriolic editorials and pamphlets issued regularly to assail the really scandalous policy of New Hampshire in refusing any of the college officers a seat in the Assembly and otherwise insulting and browbeating the " grant land " towns along the river.

When the famous Westminster Convention of

January 15, 1777, declared the territory known as the "New Hampshire Grants" a free and independent State under the name of "New Connecticut", the "College Party" was strenuous in its support and had the beatific vision of a new commonwealth, with Dresden as its capital and Dartmouth College its ruling power. In fiery opposition at once had arisen the Bennington party, under the lead of the Allens, Ethan and Ira, who termed the "College Party" as made up of "a Petulent, Pettefoging, Scribbling sort of Gentry, that will keep any government in hot water till they are thoroughly brought under by the exertions of authority." Again, the "Exeter Party", representing New Hampshire's interests in the territory, was equally offended and bitter.

When the "New Connecticut" scheme was killed by the Allens, and the State of Vermont proclaimed, Dresden and the other "grant towns" to the number of sixteen seceded from New Hampshire and joined the new commonwealth. The first Wheelock, smarting over his treatment by New Hampshire, had then asked the Vermont Assembly to take Dartmouth "under your friendly and Charitable patronage", which the Assembly proceeded to do. But the union lasted less than six months, and the "College Party" returned to its former dream of an independent State on both sides of the Connecticut.

The squabble finally reached the Continental Congress and even involved George Washington, who used his influence for the Allens and against the collegians. Eventually New Hampshire's claims as far as the Connecticut were enforced by Congress. Dresden became a part of Hanover once more, and Hanover became an intellectual capital only, with little claim to fame, save as the possessor of Dartmouth College.

Into all this turmoil, this poverty, this lack of definite policy rode the youthful soldier from the Revolutionary Army. Small wonder that he would have preferred to remain in the military service. It was not until October, 1779, that he consented to enter upon the presidency of the college, even nominally, and in September, 1780, he offered to resign. The trustees refused to hear him, and he yielded to the inevitable with something of the courage of his father and a proper respect for the *mortmain* that commanded his duty. He set to work with vigor, reorganized the faculty, and established a code of behavior for the students, who had long complained that as they were given no laws, they could not tell when they were law-breakers. This array of academic statutes included the customary amusing and snobbish specifications, as for instance:

Of their conduct and behavior towards the President

That the conduct and behaviour of the Students towards the Honourable President be in every respect with that filial duty and esteem as the importance and dignity of his station requires (viz.) uncovering their heads at and within the distance of four rods from him; also when they enter his dooryard, when the weather dont render it inconvenient and when their hands are not necessarily otherwise employed. That they never speak of him, or to him, but in a manner savory of deference and respect. That they stand when in his presence till they have permission to sit. That they wait for his liberty to speak when they would address him on any occasion. That they deliver their sentiments with modesty and propriety and deliberately. That they never contradict or enter into disputes with him; but propose their doubts grievances or arguments by way of decent interrogation. That they wait when they return an errand to him for his liberty to withdraw. That they carry their hats when they wait on him, and use no indecent gestures in his presence.

Toward the Tutors

That they treat the Tutors and Professors with a deference and respect becoming their Office and relation to them (viz.) That they uncover their heads at and within the distance of three rods from them, when the weather dont render it inconvenient, and their hands are not otherwise necessarily employed. That they enter not into controversy or dispute with them but purpose what they have to say by way of decent interrogation. That they rise when a Tutor enters the room where they are and stand till he is seated with them or they have otherwise liberty to sit. That they rise when spoken by them and never interupt them when speaking. That they be not talkative clamourous or noisy nor use indecent gestures before them. That they always carry their hats when they visit one of their rooms. That they punctually perform their orders (unless contradicted by the President) and always return their errand as soon as effected, and not withdraw without liberty.

Towards one another

That they behave with respect and kindness towards one another avoiding everything that is against the unity of the spirit or manifesting a want of friendship or contrary to the Gentleman or Christian. Junior Classes shall properly acknowledge the superiority of their Seniors by giving them the right hand in walking or sitting &c. Freshmen when in the College or in the Hall and when they speak to seniors shall have their heads uncovered and when in their company shall wait to be bidden before they cover them, unless their be such reasons to the contrary as have been mentioned. Freshmen shall at times hereafter appointed for deversion do the necessary errands for all the senior Classes who have themselves served a freshmanship (provided they are not sent more than half a mile) and shall faithfully perform and return the same.

Some laws to prevent disorder and immorality

That no student of this College be permitted to play at cards, Dice or any other unlawful game either in the

College or any other place whatever, on penalty of a fine not exceeding twenty shillings for each offense at discretion of a President or a Tutor and if persisted in they shall be expelled. That no students board at a tavern or sit at a tavern unless when on a journey or with express leave obtained for it from the President or Tutors or by desire of a Parent or Guardian, on penalty of a fine of two shillings Lawful money. And any one being convicted of a breach of this law four times within the space of six weeks shall be publicly admonished. Nor shall any student of said College be at a tavern after nine o'clock in the evening on penalty of a fine of three shillings lawful money. That no student be absent from his study after nine o'clock at night without liberty or such occasion as President or Tutors shall think sufficient on penalty of one shilling lawful money.

That no scholar send for or procure any spirituous liquors without a permit from the President or a Tutor for which he shall apply in person unless especially detained at which time he may send for one by a Freshman by whom he shall assign the reason for not comming himself; and the purpose for which he desires such permit; and such permit shall specify the time and place to which liberty is granted to have it procured.

Regulations for the security of the College building from damage

That all the students keep the rooms they respectively inhabit secure from damage. That if rooms that are unoccupied sustain special damage the cost of repairing shall be brought into contengent charges. If a student is known to have broken a window or to have done any other particular damage in the College or Hall or any

70

other public building, he shall immediately get it repaired or be at double the cost of reparation.

If any student shall play ball or use any other deversion that exposes the College or Hall windows within 3 rods of either he shall be fined two shillings for the first offense 4s for the 2d and so on at the discretion of the President or Tutors. It is earnestly recommended and injoyned upon the students that they observe neatness and cleanliness in their rooms and in their dress and avoid every practice in, upon or about the College that may be disagreeable and offensive.

But it was easier to deal with a refractory student body than with the terrors of poverty. No sooner was the Crown Prince fairly seated upon his throne, than the inevitable financial troubles began to beset him. It was evident that Dartmouth must have money, or dwindle, perhaps to the vanishing-point. The equipment was obsolete and rapidly deteriorating. The college was in debt to everybody, including the faculty and the president himself for salaries due. Notes were unpaid; provision dealers became persistent " duns ", and the credit of the college was suffering in more ways than one.

Action was imperative. The trustees decided to send the president, with our old and experienced friend, Nathaniel Whitaker, and Joseph Huntington, to foreign parts on a new begging expedition. Whitaker refused, and the matter ended in the departure of the president and his brother James in October, 1782, armed with credentials from Washington and other commanders, the President of the State and a large number of Assembly members, the French Minister, and the United States Secretary of State. They went first to France; obtained the good graces of Benjamin Franklin, proceeded to the Netherlands, and even ventured into England, in spite of the war and the prevailing hatred of Americans. They saw the Earl of Dartmouth, who expressed himself as satisfied with the work of President Wheelock, the first, but gave no encouragement in the matter of collecting new funds.

But the two must have gathered some money outside Great Britain. They set sail for home at Gravesend in early October of 1783, in the brig *Peace And Plenty*. Sardonic name! After a frightfully stormy passage across the Atlantic, which had to be interrupted by a call at Halifax for repairs, the ship was wrecked at the tip of Cape Cod, and President Wheelock, together with twoscore others, barely escaped with their lives and their clothes — nothing else. The Dartmouth " strong box ", which the president said represented five thousand pounds, was never seen again.

The trip was not wholly fruitless, however, for it

resulted in the subsequent acquisition from friends abroad of a " philosophical apparatus ", consisting of an air-pump, an orrery, a standing telescope with achromatic lenses, " an elegant set of the mechanical powers ", a thermometer and a barometer.

About this time came also from John Flude, a London broker, the curious and beautiful gold " jewel " still worn suspended from the neck of Dartmouth's president on great occasions. A little later a collection of curiosities brought to England by Captain Cook became the nucleus of the " Museum and Cabinet ", to which some kindly disposed Englishman added a stuffed zebra, long a worthy rival of Yale's two-headed snake.

These things were entertaining, but not productive. The college needed room for its young human exhibits and needed it badly. The erection of a new great hall was decided upon. The inevitable methods of the day to obtain funds were two: subscription and lottery. The first was begun energetically in March, 1784, and in a year about three thousand pounds had been subscribed. But so poverty-stricken was the college that it had to borrow ten pounds from the ever-patient John Phillips, of Exeter, in order to make a start at the new building.

The lottery was authorized by the New Hampshire Legislature in session at Portsmouth on October 30, 1784. This permitted the raising of " £3,000 L. M. in silver and gold, clear of expense, provided the same be finished within three years." The lottery was a dismal failure, due not so much to any absence of the gambling spirit in New Hampshire, as to the lack of cash to indulge it. In September, 1785, the managers made a pathetic attempt to sell the tickets for produce and grain, and about a year later asked " to be relieved from their embarrassment " by the Legislature, and were duly relieved.

Another lottery, that of September, 1787, had somewhat better success, and a drawing of the second class was held, the place being the college chapel and the instrument the desk therein. Chase says that this proceeding was " much to the scandal of some worthy people." A few of the good folk of New Hampshire must have begun to have a primordial glimmering of the fitness of things.

But with all the financial blows that fate at first gave John Wheelock, the work of setting up the new main building went bravely ahead on the site bequeathed to the college by the first president. By Commencement, 1787, it was so well along that the exercises were held in it, and it is related as an incident of that event that the official platform

Dartmouth Hall

broke down under the strain of greatness placed upon it, and that some of the solemn dignitaries " had to look for themselves in one place and for their wigs in another." In 1791, after heroic struggles to pay for the work, the building was finished. Upon it were expended in all something like £4,500, of which the lottery produced £366. The college was in debt over it for years, yet it was worth all the anxiety and trouble it caused, for it did more to stimulate the growth and reputation of the institution than any other thing of its time.

The hall was built of wood, but was large and imposing; Timothy Dwight, on his travels, reported it as of " decent " appearance, which meant more than our use of the word would indicate. It was graceful in its lines, perfect in its proportions, a beautiful piece of unconscious Colonial simplicity and good taste. When it burned in 1904, after passing safely through all the perils of open fire-places, stoves, candles, kerosene, and gas only to fall a victim to the ultra-modernity of electric wiring, the sons of the institution could hardly be blamed for feeling at first that with the passing of old Dartmouth Hall had gone also the heart of the college.

No chapel was at the outset provided for in Dartmouth Hall, and the existing place of worship in the ancient College Hall was at this time in a shocking state, so shocking that upon one dark night in 1790, the long-suffering students made a characteristic "nocturnal visitation" and tore the ramshackle structure wooden limb from wooden limb. Nobody was disciplined for this feat, and it was even hinted that the president and faculty were secretly delighted at the raid. A new chapel was built near the site of the Thornton Hall of to-day. Possibly the students may have felt that their wrecking of College Hall had been injudicious, for the new chapel was "without a chimney and never profaned by a stove", and a temperature of twenty degrees the wrong side of zero is by no means uncommon at Hanover in winter.

The college was distinctly growing under the reign of the Crown Prince. It soon rivalled any in the country as to its number of students. In 1786 it sheltered 100, in 1790 its total was 160. It graduated in 1791, with the A. B. degree, forty-nine men, to twenty-seven each at Yale, Harvard, and Princeton. In the decade 1780 to 1790, Dartmouth graduated 363 men, Harvard 394, Yale 295, and Princeton 240. Dartmouth was not then the "small college" of Webster's time.

Apparently growth in numbers was not accompanied by growth in godliness or decorum in the students. Elder Ariel Kendrick, who was a Charity

School pupil from 1785 to 1789, gives them a rather bad character. "The students at that early day", he writes, "were many of them very unruly, lawless, and without the fear of God. On a certain night they met according to agreement and prostrated the unsightly hall (the old Commons Hall), of which I have spoken, and they all soon presented to their brethren their names written in a circle. I believe they paid all the building was worth. . . .

"The number of the students at this College at this time (1847) is much larger than it was at that early day, and if they are proportionally headstrong and ungovernable, I should think the Faculty need the wisdom of Solomon, the nerves of Achilles, the patience of Job, and the meekness of Moses to manage them. . . . The stage at that time exhibited scenes wounding to Christian piety, and to which modesty was indignant. In a quarrel on the stage one would stab the other, and he would fall as dead, wallowing in blood from a concealed bladder, which was wittingly punctured by the point of the sword. A student would take the stage, assuming to be a preacher, and with a pious tone would barbecue Scripture, with a view to shower contempt upon unlearned ministers. One of these young preachers, in executing his purpose, said that 'Nebuchadnezzar's fundament was het seven times hotter than ever it was before.' Another on declamation day took the stage, dressed in a black gown, a band, and a large gray wig, with a book under his arm, and preached a sermon from the following words: ' Give me children, or else I die.' "

There can be no wonder, in the light of that testimony, that the faculty made a stringent regulation " that all dramatic exhibitions, either of a comic or a tragic nature, and spirituous liquors or representatives thereof, be wholly excluded from the stage, and that no profane or obscene expression or representation, or female habit, be introduced in any exhibition on the stage on penalty of a fine not exceeding five shillings, or admonition." Nor was piety in much better practice among the students. We are told that in the class of 1799, of which Roswell Shurtleff, afterward a famous professor of divinity, was a member, only one man publicly professed Christianity. The natural reaction came in 1801 with the establishing of the Students' Religious Society.

The consistent and unending battle with poverty, however, kept most other considerations in the background just now. John Wheelock, whatever his faults as later revealed, was no weakling. The " res angustae domi " aroused but did not terrify him. Even the loss of ten thousand dollars spent in unsuccessful defense of the college's title to the Landaff grant did not appall him. He sold twenty thousand acres of the "First College Grant", now Clarksville, at a shilling an acre, putting a thousand pounds into the treasury; a little later ten thousand acres more went for £1250.

In addition, the president bombarded the Legislature incessantly with petitions for aid. He asked for an annuity of two hundred pounds " to continue during the embarrassed condition of the College ", and again for a loan of six hundred dollars to help pay some of the institution's more pressing debts. As usual, the General Court responded by giving permission for a new lottery that should raise fifteen thousand dollars over expenses. This brought in about four thousand dollars, some eight hundred tickets having been sold in Boston alone, because Harvard was not at that time competing in the business of academic gambling. There was also some income from rents in the town of Wheelock, Vermont, a part of which had been set aside for the benefit of the Charity School in 1785.

With these aids and the Wheelock tenacity of purpose as its directing force, the college struggled on and actually grew in grace, reputation, and numbers, although from 1787 to 1803 the whole instructing body consisted of the president, two professors and one tutor. Apparently the students of that period were not averse to heckling their grave and reverend teachers. Doctor Shurtleff relates of Professor Smith:

"He was constitutionally nervous and timid. He could not well take a joke, and still less could he retort one. When a little disconcerted, he at once lost his balance, and could only receive with meekness what should come next. Having a recitation of the class of 1802 in Watts' Logic, on the doctrine of identity notwithstanding renewals of parts, one of the class, Fisk, held up his jack-knife and asked: ' If I lose this blade and get a new one, is it the same knife? ' ' Yes.' ' If I next lose the handle and get a new one, is it still the same? ' ' As a *knife* it is still the same.' ' Well, then, my chum finds the old blade and handle and puts them together, — what knife is that? ' which silenced the professor."

In 1797, the year of the founding of the Medical School, Daniel Webster entered college. He came immediately from his father's tavern and the historic hayfield, where the only way his scythe would " hang " correctly was upon the limb of a shady apple-tree. But he had had a partial " fit " at the Phillips Exeter Academy, and he never had any intellectual struggle to maintain his place in his class. He was a raw specimen when he reached

Hanover and " put up " at what is now known as the Leeds house, but then a species of tavern. In this same house, it may here be noted, Rufus Choate, the friend and compeer of Webster, was married.

The " Godlike Daniel " was not impressive as a freshman. He was thin, awkward, and so dark that one of the villagers took him for a new Indian pupil on his arrival, much to his disgust.

But he quickly made himself felt in college, though not one of his classmates would have predicted anything far out of the common for him. He had personality, and he could make speeches in a somewhat better style than the dull, sophomoric manner of the day — that much they felt sure of. In his senior year he delivered an eulogy of his classmate Simonds, which his room-mate Aaron Loveland afterward said " was very good, but produced no extraordinary effect." A sample is quite sufficient to show its crudities of expression: " The sun, as it sinks to the ocean, plays its departing beams on his tomb, but they re-animate him not. The cold sod presses on his bosom, his hands hang down in weakness. The bird of evening shouts a melancholy air on the poplar, but her voice is stillness to his ears."

In his junior year, Webster gave the Fourth of

July oration to the citizens of Hanover. This was a more finished product, but still marked by extravagances. He termed Napoleon "the gasconading pilgrim of Egypt" and declared that France, "not yet satisfied with the contortions of expiring republics, spouted her fury across the Atlantic!" It was a long distance from that sort of thing to the reply to Hayne; but Webster was yet a boy of eighteen. The beginnings of the orator were stirring within him.

The college life of "Black Dan" was not particularly eventful. He seems to have behaved rather better than the times demanded; flirted a little with the "college widows"; drank moderately enough, so far as there is any record; studied honestly and easily; talked in public and in his literary society, the United Fraternity, on all possible occasions and wrote poems and skits for the *Dartmouth Gazette*, receiving in all about seventy-five dollars, enough to pay a whole year's board in that glad day of moderate prices. He afterwards wrote of himself at this period:

"Of my college life I can say but little. I was graduated, in course, in August, 1801. Owing to some difficulties, *haec non meminisse juvat*, I took no part in the Commencement exercises. I spoke an oration to the Society of the United Fraternity, which

I suspect was a sufficiently boyish performance. My college life was not an idle one. Besides the regular attendance of prescribed duties and studies, I read something of English history and English literature. Perhaps my reading was too miscellaneous. I even paid my board for a year by superintending a little weekly newspaper, and making selections for it from books of literature, and from the contemporary publications. I suppose I sometimes wrote a foolish paragraph myself.

" While in College I delivered two or three occasional addresses, which were published. I trust they are forgotten; they were in very bad taste. I had not then learned that all true power in writing is in the idea, not in the style, an error into which the *ars rhetorica*, as it is usually taught, may easily lead stronger heads than mine."

At another time Webster was not so humble. Professor Sanborn, dining with him at Franklin one day, observed: " It is commonly reported that you did not study much in College." We are told that the " Godlike " replied angrily: " What fools they must be to suppose that anybody could succeed in college or public life without study! I studied and read more than all the rest of my class, if they had all been made into one man. And I was as much above them then as I am now." Whether that was the simple and natural egoism of great genius or the promptings of another sort of inspiration, Webster later wrote that " my scholarship was overestimated. Many other students read more than I did and knew more than I did ", and he told George Ticknor: " My Greek and Mathematics were not great while I was in College, but I was better read in history and English generally than any of my class, and I was good in composition. My Latin was pretty strong, too."

Judge Loveland in 1857 gave the most pungent estimate of Webster as a collegian that can be found anywhere. " I roomed with Webster ", said he, " about one year. He was very ambitious in college from the first, and took every opportunity to make himself conspicuous. He had unbounded self-confidence, seemed to feel that a good deal belonged to him, and evidently intended to be a great man in public life. He was rather bombastic and always ready for a speech. One day he was reading Addison's ' Cato,' putting it off in great style, when he pronounced ' Utica ' as if the first letter was short; I corrected him, and he said I was right. He did a great deal in his college society, and received almost unbounded flattery from his fellow-members. They thought he was great. It was common for others to say they overestimated him. He was not very popular with the class, owing to his being so independent and assuming.

"On one occasion, when some matter was discussed before the class, the side which he advocated received but few votes, whereupon he got up and left the room. He would appear rather stuffy if things did not go to suit him, though he took no special pains at electioneering. On the whole, he was regarded as our ablest man; if anything was to be done he was generally appointed. He never refused; would always take hold and get off something, and generally did well. He came to college from a tavern kept by his father, who was in embarrassed circumstances. His father was at our room while we were together. He said that if he had received education in youth, he could have done anything he chose.

"Dan was rough and awkward, very decidedly, and I sometimes doubted whether he would succeed in life on that account. Yet there was something rather assuming and pompous in his bearing as well as his style. He observed things remarkably, and was quick to see their bearings. He was, and felt himself to be, a kind of oracle. He read the newspapers and kept himself posted upon political affairs remarkably for a young man. He read a good deal also of general reading. If any distinguished men were about, he would manage to fall in with them; met more than most students, and was distinguished in the community around the College, for the extent and readiness of his political knowledge. He was a good, though not a very accurate scholar. He would occasionally come over here to Norwich, Saturdays, to hunt with me. Dan seldom hit anything."

The hoary, but still extant bit of fiction that Webster, after receiving his diploma, went out behind Dartmouth Hall and tore the document to pieces because he had not been given the valedictory oration, shouting as he performed the deed: " My industry may make me a great man, but this miserable parchment cannot ", should be given an unhonored burial and not resurrected. It has no basis in fact, in the testimony of classmates, in the character of the man, or in his love for the college, which he frequently revisited soon after leaving it, and to which he sent his brother and his son. He was disappointed and grieved, but he did not act like an ingrate or a fool.

The facts were that Thomas A. Merrill, " the most correct recitation scholar in the class ", was awarded the salutatory, at that time the chief Commencement prize. The class was asked to elect the valedictorian, but it failed to do so on account of a bitter quarrel between the members of the United Fraternity and the Social Friends. It is said that the students desired and expected the faculty to choose Webster, but that body gave that part to Caleb Tenney and offered Webster his choice between an English poem or an English oration, neither of which the offended Daniel would take. "The faculty", wrote Merrill afterward, "thought it would be almost barbarous to set the best English scholar in the class to jabber in Latin."

Thus went out from his "cherishing mother" the greatest figure she has sent into the world. If there was a cloud of dissatisfaction over his exit, affairs were even then so shaping themselves that it was soon to be lifted and reveal the man himself in the sunlight of his fame and his powers, fighting the winning battle that saved for his college her very life itself.

CHAPTER VI

THE GREAT "CASE"

JOHN WHEELOCK'S energy and executive ability of a certain sort, reflected by the self-evident growth of the college through his long reign, was sufficient for many years to still the sporadic mutterings against the family dynasty, within and without. For almost a generation there was nothing that the hostiles could do, except mutter and try to block the attempts of the college to obtain a crumb or two from the legislative table. Wheelock was a man of determination, and in his Hanoverian castle were for some time his own family retainers. Doctor Benjamin Pomeroy, one of the charter members of the board of trustees, was an uncle by marriage. Bezaleel Woodward, another trustee, was his brother-in-law. Sylvanus Ripley was still another who filled both functions.

The remaining trustees, who lived at a distance, were not often at meetings of the board, for a trip to Hanover over the still fearsome roads was unattractive. The dynasty trustees, themselves ruled by Wheelock, naturally regulated matters to suit their liege. The faculty was Wheelock through and through, consisting of two sons and two sons-in-law of Eleazar, with the fifth man, Professor Smith, practically a member of the family.

These conditions changed with time, but for the first years of his reign, Prince John governed Dartmouth as an absolute monarch, firm in his belief that as his father had been the college, so was he by divine right and human testament. For that principle he was willing to fight at any time, and fight he had to with the waxing of the new century.

Gradually there arose from the necessities brought about by the deaths of the older members, a board of trustees that knew not Eleazar and began to dare to question the edicts of his son. The new notion of taking their duties and responsibilities seriously gradually grew among them. In 1804 but one member of the original board was left. John Wheelock could no longer play Hamlet with the ghost of his father and expect to see it potent. In minor ways the trustees began to make this evident.

It was, however, one of those religious squabbles, not uncommon in the early history of many colleges, that finally involved the president and his board of trustees in an open and bitter warfare that was not to cease until it reached the greatest tribunal of the world as its greatest case up to that time and argued by the greatest forensic lawyer of his day. From the small white church that now stands in such demure simplicity at the northwestern end of the campus, came the discordant elements, as from an ecclesiastical Pandora's box, that raged for years and nearly killed the college.

The house of worship, whose walls rang with the Commencement eloquence of every class from 1796 to 1907, was built in 1795 at a cost of about five thousand dollars. It was the property of " The Church of Christ at Dartmouth College ", not of the college itself, although the trustees promised that they would, in better financial weather, make up a part of the cost and would meantime pay for the college use of it. The proprietors before long began to look for the rental. It was slow in coming. Finally the trustees voted that " each member of the College shall pay one dollar on the second Wednesday in March for preaching and the use of seats in the meeting house for the ensuing year."

This tax President Wheelock passed on to the undergraduates, and their indignation knew no bounds. It was bad enough, they protested, to be compelled to listen to Professor Smith's preaching without being made to pay for the ordeal. So much of a storm arose that the trustees soon revoked the

College Church

order. The president then seceded from the church, taking all the students and Professor Smith to the college chapel for Sunday services; this in the face of the agreement of the trustees to compensate the religious society for the attendance of the students and the damage they should do to the pews, which, judging from some venerable relics still extant thirty years ago, was considerable.

The trouble was adjudicated in 1798, and the students went back, with their jack-knives, to the church. But it had served to arouse among the trustees a fear that the domination of the president was not altogether for the best.

Soon came another long church imbroglio over the question of pastor. Wheelock insisted upon his amiable echo, Doctor Smith. Whereupon the Hanover men for the most part quit the old church and organized "The Congregation in the Vicinity of Dartmouth College" with Professor Shurtleff as its minister.

The meeting-house was used by both factions at different hours, and there is on record no story of any clashes more serious than those of words. Wheelock's anger took the form of several attempts upon the trustees to get them to forbid Shurtleff to preach for the new church, charging him with neglect of his college duties. The board was by this time more Congregationalist than Presbyterian, and it refused. At the meeting of August 27, 1811, it drew up a statement concluding with these words:

"The trustees have long labored to restore the harmony which formerly prevailed in this Institution, without success: and it is with reluctance they express their apprehension, that if the present state of things is suffered to remain any great length of time, the College will be essentially injured."

That may be set down as the first official notice to John Wheelock that he would have a fight on his hands if he did not mend his cantankerous ways. The trustees had reached the point where, as one of them said, they were no longer willing that even the son of his father should be " the *omnis homo* of the College." They began to pass laws curbing his powers. He retorted that they were guilty of usurpation and perversion of funds.

The first shot of the great contest was fired from ambuscade, and took the form of a paragraph in the *Boston Repertory*, of April 26, 1815, stating that as a result of " difficulties of a serious and unpleasant nature ", the president of Dartmouth College might be expected to resign shortly, and that the trustees and alumni were looking about for his successor.

As this was what John Wheelock had no remotest intention of doing, the effect on him may be imagined. He had the *Dartmouth Gazette* say that the item was " a gross and infamous misrepresentation ", and followed up this retort by the publication of an anonymous pamphlet entitled " Sketches of the History of Dartmouth College and Moor's Charity School ", accompanied by another called " A Candid and Analytical Review " of the former. The president wrote the first, and his friend, Reverend Elijah Parish, of Byfield, Massachusetts, the second. Both were vitriolic in their denunciations of the trustees, whom they accused of subordinating the interests of the college to their religious prejudices, the inference being that Wheelock was liberal and the board a set of hard-shelled ecclesiastical Tories.

The newspapers promptly jumped into the fray, the *Concord Patriot*, the *Portsmouth Gazette* and the *Windsor* (Vt.) *Washingtonian* supporting Wheelock, and the *Concord Gazette*, the *Portsmouth Oracle* and the *Dartmouth Gazette* lining up for the trustees. Soon the quarrel became political, with the Federalists in general on the side of the trustees, and the Democrats espousing the cause of the president. In a few months the fight was an issue at the polls, and the members of the Legislature were elected as Wheelockites or anti-Wheelockites.

In June, 1815, the beleaguered president applied to the Legislature for help, now alleging that the trustees were scheming " to strengthen the interest of a party or sect, which by extending its influence under the fairest professions, will eventually affect the political independence of the people, and move the springs of their government."

This arrant nonsense and characteristic bombast must have been regarded seriously by the solons, for a committee was appointed to hear Wheelock's plea. He asked for legislation to enlarge the board of trustees, so that his enemies would be outnumbered, promising to leave half his estate to the college if that were done. The Legislature replied by appointing a committee to go to Hanover and investigate. The session was fixed for August 16. Wheelock immediately sent for Mr. Webster, whom he had retained after a fashion some months before to represent him in case of trouble. But the message reached Portsmouth too late, and Webster, as it appeared from a letter to one Dunham, who had attacked him viciously for alleged breach of good faith, would not have come in any event.

" If I had received it earlier," he wrote, " I could not have attended, because the court engaged me at home; and I ought to add here, that if I had no other engagements at the time, and had also been seasonably notified, I should have exercised my own discretion about undertaking to act a part before the committee at Hanover. I regard that as no professional call. . . . I am not quite so fully convinced as you are, that the president is altogether right, and the trustees altogether wrong."

That disposes of the assertion that Webster betrayed Wheelock and shifted his opinions to suit the political winds. It is evident that he was not on the president's side at any time after the real lines of the struggle had been drawn.

On the assembling of the investigators, Wheelock immediately presented his case against the trustees, charging them, among other things, with:

Separating the church founded in College, and blending the ecclesiastical concerns of the College with those of the neighboring people and clergy; thus subjecting this public institution to inconvenience and degradation, by means of private interference.

Expending the funds to an amount unnecessary and extravagant, compared with the sum total of instruction.

Refusing to apply any of the funds, of which they have control, to the instruction of Indians.

Interfering with the power of the President, as granted by charter, in the education of the students, and also with his rights, as an executive officer.

To this the gentlemen responded rather feebly, so far as their appearance before the committee was concerned; but they acted vigorously enough. Wheelock was declared to be and denounced as the author of the seditious " Sketches." The president replied with an ungrammatical and pompous blast of defiance, refusing to meet with the board and denying its jurisdiction. Its counter-thrust was startling: Wheelock was deposed. At six in the morning of August 26, the trustees met and voted the Crown Prince's academic execution, with resolutions charging him with libel on the college; with usurpation of the whole executive authority; with fraud in the application of the funds of Moor's School by passing off a white man as an Indian; and with lying as to the cause of the contest. Thus they concluded:

They consider this crisis as a severe trial to the institution, but they believe that in order to entertain a hope that it will flourish and be useful, they must be faithful to their trust, — that they must not approve of an officer who labors to destroy its reputation, and embarrass its eternal concerns. They will yet hope that under the smiles of Divine Providence this institution will continue to flourish, and be a great blessing to generations to come.

Therefore, Resolved that the appointment of Dr. John Wheelock to the presidency of this college by the last will of the Rev. Eleazar Wheelock, the founder and first President of this College, be and the same is hereby, by the trustees of said College, disapproved, and it is further Resolved that the said Dr. John Wheelock for the reason aforesaid, be and he is hereby displaced and removed from the office of President of said College.

On the same morning the board chose Reverend Francis Brown, 1805, of Yarmouth, Maine, president in Wheelock's place. The latter immediately wrote the Maine clergyman that in his view the action of the trustees was illegal and void; but Mr. Brown was inaugurated as president on the twenty-seventh of September.

Now ensued a civil war within the confines at Hanover, the like of which no college town in America has ever seen. The Democrats won the next election and, with Governor Plumer and the Legislature partisans of Wheelock, it was easy to obtain the enactment of a bill changing the name of the college to Dartmouth University, increasing the number of trustees to twenty-one, and establishing a board of overseers of twenty-five, including, *ex officio*, the Governor and Council, the President of the Senate and Speaker of the House, and the Governor and Lieutenant-Governor of Vermont. These boards made Wheelock president of the university.

The trustees of the college declined to take places in the new board. But Judge Woodward, the secretary and treasurer, went over to the enemy, carrying with him the Great Seal and the records and the college property, which he refused to surrender. This seeming misfortune turned out to be the real foundation for the suit at law which proved the salvation of the college.

To add to the difficulties of the trustees, the Legislature passed a bill of penalties providing that any person assuming to perform the duties of president, trustee, or any officer of the college, except in conformity to the acts of the Legislature, should forfeit for each offense five hundred dollars, to be recovered by any person who should sue therefor, one half to go to the complainant and one half to the university. President Brown, with all his gentleness and culture, had plenty of steel under his velvet exterior, and he declined to be frightened. As a matter of fact, no action was ever taken under this penal law.

In the midst of the turmoil, John Wheelock fell a victim to " a dropsy of the chest " and died, on April 4, 1817, at the age of sixty-three. He had lived many years too long for the good of his fame. The qualities of fearlessness, energy, and undoubted devotion to the college which did such excellent service in the first half of his administration, became obstinacy, autocracy and almost incredible vanity in the last half. Nor was he shrewd enough to mitigate his domineering by any claims to partnership with the Almighty, as his father had done. Possibly the era was too late for the success of that sort of thing.

THE GREAT "CASE"

He lacked culture and in his writings was turgid and almost illiterate. Lord relates that his prayers at chapel were marvels of grotesque taste. " Having one day chanced to attend to some experiment in the chemistry of gases, he thanked the Lord in his next chapel prayer for the elements in detail: ' We thank thee O Lord for the oxygen gas; we thank thee O Lord for the hydrogen gas; we thank thee O Lord for the nitrogen gas and for all the gases.' At another time he was impressed in the same way by the wonders of anatomy and expressed his gratitude in like form ' for the cerebrum, for the cerebellum and for the medulla oblongata.' "

A composite by two of the students who took the trouble to write of him afterward furnishes as accurate a picture of John Wheelock as the world of to-day cares for. Thus Stephen Farley, of the class of 1804:

It was his habit to speak in a stiff and affectedly elevated style; to assume some empirical airs of the polite gentleman; to exact attention from others and to pay for them by making superfluous bows, and lighting up his face with smiles, while he gracefully lifted and waved his tri-cornered beaver. Notwithstanding the stilt-walking character of his style he acquitted himself well in his lectures, which were always unwritten.

In personal presence he made in his prime a good appearance. His stature was of the average, his shoulders rather broad, and he was very erect. He had a light complexion; abundant brown hair, clubbed behind, and parted in the middle of the forehead. His nose was large and aquiline; his eyes bright, and his eyebrows and mouth rather uncommonly elongated.

He wore a dun colored coat as often as a black one; and always small clothes and white stockings; and, when the weather required, a drab double-breasted great coat. The barber visited his study twice a week, and so at prayers on Wednesday and Saturday evenings he appeared all shaven and shorn with a sprinkling of powder on the crown of his head.

George Ticknor, 1807, gave this as his contribution:

Doctor Wheelock was stiff and stately. He read constantly, sat up late and got up early. He talked very gravely and slow, with a falsetto voice. Mr. Webster could imitate him perfectly. . . . He was one of the most formal men I ever knew. I saw a great deal of him from 1802 to 1816 in his own house and my father's, but never felt the smallest degree of familiarity with him, nor do I believe that any of the students did. They were generally very awkward, unused to the ways of the world. Many of them when they went to the President on their little affairs did not know when the time had come for them to get up and leave him. He was very covetous of his time, and when the business was settled, and he had waited a little while he would say, " Will you sit longer, or will you go now? " It was a recognized formula, and no young man that I ever knew of, ever sat longer after hearing it.

Perhaps it is as well to take leave of the second president with the thought that he was courteous, at any rate. Lord says " he had pleasant personal qualities and had some devoted friends and supporters." In the life of Doctor A. Alexander we find that " It was pleasantly said that he suffered no man to have the last bow. This, it was reported, was put to the test by a person of some assurance who undertook to compete with him in a contest of politeness. He accordingly took his leave, bowed himself out of the mansion, and continued to bow as long as he was upon the premises, but the President followed him to the gate, and remained in possession of the field."

When Wheelock passed out of the fight for the academic control of Hanover, and William Allen, of Pittsfield, Massachusetts, came into it as president of Dartmouth University there was still something of the dynasty tinge to the succession, for Allen was Wheelock's son-in-law. But he was an amiable gentleman and went through his difficult rôle with as little offense as possible.

The two institutions by the name of Dartmouth on Hanover plain proceeded for a while under an understood truce. The university had the buildings, which they seized with the aid of a couple of village " huskies ", but the college had the students, who stood loyally by to the number of 130, while their rivals were so few that they were ashamed to get out a catalogue. President Brown hired a hall over Stewart's hat store for use as a chapel and for senior recitations, while the lower classes met in various student's rooms. But " we all followed one bell ", wrote Nathan Crosby in his " First Half Century of Dartmouth College ", " and for two long years a hundred or more students were crossing the plain, at every ringing of the bell, to their chapel and various recitation rooms, while a dozen university students were crossing our paths in other directions, giving ample opportunity to crack a joke and chaff each other."

Henry K. Oliver says much the same thing: "There was, by a sort of tacit consent, a general harmony between the several students. The same tintinnabulum summoned both parties to prayers, recitations, and meals, and they crossed the same campus; yet not without a muchness of good-natured chaff and banter, we the ' hoi polloi ', and they the ' few yet brave.' "

The first Commencements under the dual system were held on the same day, August 27, 1817. Each party claimed the church for its exercises. The pewholders disagreed. General Poole, Colonel Brewster, and Colonel Perkins, of the university persuasion, swore they would call out the militia to support President Allen, whereupon a party of sixty college students took possession of the sacred edifice by night and held it for three days, armed with canes and clubs and provided with stones to hurl from the belfry upon the heads of university invaders. President Brown offered to compromise by giving the university the auditorium after one o'clock on Commencement day, but President Allen refused to yield precedence and held the Commencement in the chapel in the college yard, graduating eight men to the college's thirty-nine.

Manifestly it was impossible for two sets of college boys, lively young Americans of that rather "cocky" period after the war of 1812, to get on in such strange fashion without at least one serious clash. The wonder is that riot was not frequent, instead of nearly unknown. The one example was sufficiently exhilarating.

The university people had early seized the college library, amounting to about four thousand volumes, and the student societies, the United Fraternity and the Social Friends, feared that their books would likewise be carried off. Each appointed a Committee of Safety. Rufus Choate, then librarian of the Socials, hired a room in Professor Adams' house, where he lived, and under cover of darkness superintended the removal of a part of the Socials' library to that hiding-place and the packing of the rest in trunks ready for quick transfer. The United Fraternity men also removed some of their books.

Cautious as these manoeuvres were, news of them in some way filtered through to the university administration. President Allen, on the eleventh of November, ordered Henry Hutchinson, the inspector of buildings, to take and hold the library room of the two societies. This functionary collected a *posse comitatus* made up of Professors Dean and Carter, five students of the university, and eight " townies."

The procession moved in force against the quarters of the Socials, trying to break in the door by a human battering-ram. This failing, one Coffin, a villager, was ordered to cut an entrance with his axe. The din was terrific, arousing the students living near by, and bringing the members of the United Fraternity, who were holding a meeting in the hall below, to the rescue in a wild rush. Seeing the invaders armed, the " Fraters " laid hold on some cordwood sticks piled in the corridor.

Henry K. Oliver, afterward famous as the composer of *Federal Street* and other popular hymn-tunes, who was gifted with a voice like a mellifluous fog-horn, dashed down the stairways and into the open in front of the hall, where he bellowed with all his might: "Turn out, Social Friends, your library is broken open." The campus was in an uproar in an instant, — across the paths came running the frenzied college men, to the accompaniment of a wild alarum from the cupola bell, which some of the society defenders were ringing as if half the world were on fire. Nesmith, of the class of 1820, thus described the scene:

We heard Oliver's ringing voice distinctly at our room. Chamberlain (afterwards professor), who was then librarian of the Fraternity and roomed directly over me, was soon in my room, seeking a light, at the head of the body of his society, who immediately commenced the labor of removing the remaining books of their library to the hall of Dr. Alden. I was soon at the scene of action at the other end of the building, where we found Coffin still cutting away the door, and Hutchinson giving orders. Professors Dean and Carter were also present, with Bissell and Cook and three shoemakers and others unknown to fame. The first sensible speech I heard was from one of the shoemakers who addressed his associates saying, " it appears to me we are in a cursed poor scrape. I had rather be in a nest of hornets than among these college boys when they get mad and roused up."

The university men had cut a hole in the Socials' door large enough to admit them one by one, and they were now inside, holding the breach with their axe, and declaring that no Social could remove a single book and live to tell the tale. But no blood was spilt, for the university crowd, finding itself overwhelmingly outnumbered, surrendered gracefully and submitted to imprisonment in an adjacent room until the society adherents had removed all their books. President Allen had nine of the college boys arrested for riot, among them " R. Choate." They retaliated by swearing out warrants against Professors Dean and Carter and some others of the university raiders. No one was indicted, and the excitement died out almost as suddenly as it had arisen.

All this time the great " Case " had been steadily in the making, and with a trend adverse to the college. Helped incalculably by the gift of one thousand dollars from John B. Wheeler, of Orford, New Hampshire, without whose money the fight would not have been made,[1] the trustees brought suit of trover against Treasurer Woodward to recover the seal, the charter, the records, and the accounts,

---

[1] In November, 1817, President Brown appealed to Harvard for financial aid in a cause common to all the chartered colleges. President Kirkland replied that he was in full sympathy with Dartmouth, but that Harvard had no funds for the purpose of helping the legal battle, adding also that his friends and advisers feared that the college would be beaten in the United States Supreme Court, which would make the situation of Harvard and the other colleges precarious. Dartmouth fought out the cause of the rest single-handed.

Wheeler Hall

which he had carried over to the university, all to the alleged value of fifty thousand dollars.

The first argument of the case was made at Haverhill in the spring of 1817. Those intellectual giants, Jeremiah Mason and Jeremiah Smith, appeared for the college, while George Sullivan and Ichabod Bartlett, both keen and able pleaders, were for the university. The case was continued to the September sitting at Exeter, and there Webster joined the others, making the closing plea for the college. The counsel on this side argued that the acts of the Legislature of New Hampshire were not obligating:

1. Because they are not within the general scope of legislative power.

2. Because they violate certain provisions of the Constitution of this State, restraining the legislative power.

3. Because they violate the Constitution of the United States.

To these claims Sullivan and Bartlett replied that the college, being a public corporation, was intended for the benefit of the public and of those composing it, and that while the contention of the plaintiffs might apply to Moor's Charity School, it did not apply to Dartmouth College, and that the grant did not come within the meaning of the "obligation" clause of the Constitution of the United States. The court, in spite of the statement that it was left in tears by Webster's eloquence, decided in favor of the university. Webster had expected this. " It would be queer ", he had said, " if Governor Plumer's court did not sustain his own law."

The " Case " next moved on to Washington. By agreement of both sides, the New Hampshire court rendered a special verdict carrying it directly to the Supreme Court, on the sole point that the Legislature had violated the Constitution by " impairing the obligations of contracts." The matter came up for argument on March 10, 1815. Mason and Smith did not appear, but Webster was aided by Joseph Hopkinson, of Philadelphia, now best known to fame as the author of *Hail Columbia*, but a great jurist in his day.

The university was clearly outclassed, with John Holmes, a Maine lawyer of political proclivities, and William Wirt, the amiable builder of florid word-pictures, who was then attorney-general of the United States, pitted against " Black Dan." Yet the latter's task was herculean, and he knew it. Chief Justice Marshall and one associate were believed favorable to the college; two others were known to be hostile. The other three were undecided in their views; two of them must be won, and

Mr. Webster set all of his mighty powers to winning them.

Of that historic scene in the old Supreme Court room in the Senate wing of the basement of the Capitol, Chauncey A. Goodrich, professor of oratory at Yale, who went to Washington for the express purpose of hearing Webster, has left the best description in a letter sent afterward to Rufus Choate. Thus he wrote:

Mr. Webster entered upon his argument in the calm tone of easy and dignified conversation. His matter was so completely at his command that he scarcely looked at his brief, but went on for more than four hours with a statement so luminous, and a chain of reasoning so easy to be understood, and yet approaching so nearly to absolute demonstration, that he seemed to carry with him every man of his audience, without the slightest effort or uneasiness on either side. It was hardly eloquence, in the strict sense of the term: it was pure reason. Now and then for a sentence or two his eye flashed and his voice swelled into a bolder note, as he uttered some emphatic thought, but he instantly fell back into the tone of earnest conversation, which ran throughout the great body of his speech. A single circumstance will show the clearness and absorbing power of his argument. I observed Judge Story sit, pen in hand, as if to take notes. Hour after hour I saw him fixed in the same attitude; but I could not discover that he made a single note. The argument ended, Mr. Webster stood for some moments silent before the court, while every eye was fixed intently upon him. At length, addressing Chief Justice Marshall, he said, —

"*This, sir, is my case.* It is the case, not merely of that humble institution, it is the case of every college in our land. It is more. It is the case of every eleemosynary institution throughout our country, of all those great charities founded by the piety of our ancestors to alleviate human misery, and scatter blessings along the pathway of human life. It is more. It is, in some sense, the case of every man who has property of which he may be stripped, — for the question is simply this: Shall our State legislatures be allowed to take that which is not their own, to turn it from its original use, and apply it to such ends or purposes as they, in their discretion, shall see fit? Sir, you may destroy this little institution; it is weak; it is in your hands! I know it is one of the lesser lights in the literary horizon of our country. You may put it out; but if you do, you must carry through your work! You must extinguish, one after another, all those great lights of science which, for more than a century, have thrown their radiance over the land! It is, sir, as I have said, a small college, *and yet there are those that love it* — "

Here the feelings which he had thus far succeeded in keeping down, broke forth. His lips quivered; his firm cheeks trembled with emotion; his eyes were filled with tears; his voice choked, and he seemed struggling to the utmost, simply to gain the mastery over himself which might save him from an unmanly burst of feeling. I will not attempt to give you the few broken words of tenderness in which he went on to speak of his attachment to the College. The whole seemed to be mingled with the recollections of father, mother, brother, and all the privations through which he had made his way into life. Every one saw that it was wholly unpremeditated, — a pressure on his heart which sought relief in words and tears.

The court-room during these two or three minutes presented an extraordinary spectacle. Chief Justice Marshall, with his tall, gaunt figure bent over as if to catch the slightest whisper, the deep furrows of his cheek expanded with emotion, and eyes suffused with tears; Mr. Justice Washington at his side, with his small and emaciated frame, and countenance more like marble than I ever saw on any other human being, leaning forward with an eager, troubled look; and the remainder of the court at the two extremities, pressing, as it were, toward a single point, while the audience below were wrapping themselves round in closer folds beneath the bench to catch each look, and every movement of the speaker's face. . . . There was not one among the strong-minded men of that assembly who could think it unmanly to weep, when he saw standing before him the man who had made such an argument melted into the tenderness of a child.

Mr. Webster, having recovered his composure and fixed his keen eye upon the Chief Justice, said, in that deep tone with which he sometimes thrilled the heart of an audience, —

" Sir, I know not how others may feel " (glancing at the opponents of the College before him, some of whom were its graduates), " but, for myself, when I see my alma mater surrounded, like Cæsar in the senate house, by those who are reiterating stab upon stab, I would not, for this right hand, have her turn to me and say, *Et tu quoque, mi fili! — And thou too, my son!* "

He sat down; there was a deathlike stillness throughout the room for some moments; every one seemed to be slowly recovering himself and coming gradually back to his ordinary range of thought and feeling.

After this tremendous emotional appeal, backed by the keenest legal knowledge of the subject, the arguments of Holmes for the university fell flat. He stumbled into bad errors of judgment and showed ignorance of the case. Webster was human enough to gloat. "I had a malicious joy," he wrote to Judge Smith, "in seeing Judge Bell sit by to hear him, while everybody was grinning at the folly he uttered. Bell could not stand it. He seized his hat and went off."

Wirt ruined whatever effect he might have produced by the idiotic admission that he "had not had time to study the case and had hardly thought of it till it was called on." Hopkinson is said to have made "a calm and able" closing for the college. But it was the master mind and organ tones of Webster that ruled the court alone and won the decision for Dartmouth College and so many other American colleges.

This case, stubbornly fought to its victorious end by the poor and small institution at Hanover, fought when compromise would have been easy and pleasant, has been more often cited in our courts

than any other. According to Chancellor Kent:
"The decision in that case did more than any other
single act proceeding from the authority of the
United States to throw an impregnable barrier
around all rights and franchises derived from the
grant of government; and to give solidity and in-
violability to the literary, charitable, religious, and
commercial institutions of our country."

In the opinion of Henry Cabot Lodge, the decision
was "in its effects more far-reaching and of more
general interest than perhaps any other ever made
in this country."

The verdict of the tribunal at Washington was
announced on February 2, 1818. Only one justice,
Duvall, dissented. It took a week for the news to
reach Hanover. Then "the expressions of joy were
excessive." Cannon boomed for two days, and it
is hinted by the local chroniclers that the celebration
was more spirituous than spiritual. The college
men seized all the buildings, and at the beginning
of the spring term, President Allen announced that
there would be no more instruction in the university. He had received shabby treatment by the
Legislature in return for his loyal service. His
salary was supposed to be twelve hundred dollars
a year, but he was paid only $983 for his two years'
work, and the very body that had set him up in

the university refused to do anything more for him. It is not difficult to guess what would have happened to Dartmouth had Daniel Webster failed her at Washington.

When the decision that killed the university and left it unwept, save by a lot of New Hampshire politicians, was made public at Washington, Judge Hopkinson wrote to President Brown: "The court goes all lengths with us, and whatever trouble the gentlemen may give us in future, they cannot shake those principles which must and will restore Dartmouth College to its true and original owners. I would have an inscription over the door of your building, — '*Founded by Eleazar Wheelock, Refounded by Daniel Webster.*'"

At the portals of Webster Hall, the dignified and handsome memorial built by the alumni at the northeast corner of the campus, the words suggested by Hopkinson are written in enduring bronze.

Webster Hall

CHAPTER VII

DANA AND TYLER

WHEN the great " Case " had ended, Dartmouth College was Dartmouth College still, but it was like an exhausted army, victorious, yet shot almost to pieces. It had its property again; the Great Seal had been dragged out from the grain bin, where the widow of Treasurer Woodward had hidden it against theft or mutilation, and restored to its owners; a jubilee had been made of the Commencement of 1819, with Webster an idolized figure, and the eminent counsel formally thanked by the trustees and asked to sit for their portraits. There was, of course, much cause for rejoicing.

But clouds of anxiety and even distress hung over the institution. The university faction of the press was bitter in its defeat. Isaac Hill declared in the *New Hampshire Register* that " by this decision it is to be understood that the people of New Hampshire as a State have no longer an interest in Dartmouth College." A movement to establish a rival " public literary Institution " on the part of the State actually made some headway in the

Legislature, and a little later a "Literary Fund" was voted, to be raised by a stamp tax on bank circulation, for the future endowment of a university.

Some of the college people in the Legislature, thinking that they might divert this financial aid to Dartmouth by agreeing to the creation of a State board of overseers "somewhat on the footing of Cambridge", consulted Webster on the matter. He was thoroughly against it.

"I wish," he wrote, "I had more hope of good than I have to the College from the Legislature. Of course you know best the feeling on such subjects at present existing, but for myself I do not believe the College could get a dollar from the Gen. Court."

Lack of money was again the besetting peril to the college. During the fight with New Hampshire it had lost its student rental for rooms and its income from lands. The expenses of the suit were about six thousand dollars, and to add to the trouble the heirs of President John Wheelock brought suit for the collection of $7,886 unpaid salary and ten thousand dollars for "the work, labor, care, and diligence" of the son of his father as head of the college. A settlement was finally made for $8,385, which kept the institution in debt for years. Besides, it owed its own officers nearly five thousand dollars in unpaid salaries. The trustees tried to get indemnity from the Legislature for their losses incurred by the university fiasco; it can readily be imagined that their plea was extinguished with ribald laughter in that still unregenerate body.

A very real disaster following close upon the heels of these troubles was the death, on July 27, 1820, of President Brown. He had literally worn himself out in the struggle, and he paid the penalty of his devotion at thirty-six. His brief, but terribly difficult administration shows him to have been a rare soul. " In person ", says Lord, " he was unusually dignified and commanding, yet natural and graceful in carriage. His large, full hazel eye, and genial, beaming face invited confidence, but his expression was so penetrating and sagacious as to forbid deception, and repel familiarity. When the occasion required he could be terribly severe, but this severity had nothing of personal anger in it. To govern young men was natural and easy to him. He rarely used the language of command. A wish or request expressed in the mildest form was with the students equivalent to a command, and was promptly regarded. He was both honored and loved. The discipline of the College was never more perfect than during the years when the laws of the College were stript of authority, when the students were under the ban of the legislature and when each student knew that his course might end without academic honors. The main influence in holding the College together was the personality of the President."

President Brown's successor was the Reverend Doctor Daniel Dana, of Newburyport, Massachusetts; a successful preacher and a man of evident common sense, which he reluctantly allowed to be overruled by his Presbytery, to which was referred the pressing call of the Dartmouth trustees. He has the historic distinction of one of the briefest administrations on record among the colleges. Inaugurated on October 3, 1820, he resigned within six months, a prey to melancholia. His letter to the trustees declaring his withdrawal reveals a man who knew what a college president should be, even if he could not himself be one. " The College needs a President ", he wrote, " not only of powerful talents, but of strong nerves and vigorous health; one who can enterprise much and accomplish much; one whom labors cannot easily exhaust nor difficulties embarrass, nor trials depress. In reference to all these particulars I have a painful consciousness, I will not say of *deficiency*, but of *contrast*."

Then followed Reverend Bennett Tyler, a parson

of South Britain, Connecticut, and a Yale man of 1804. He, too, hesitated over the offer, preferring the life of a country clergyman. He, too, was persuaded by a religious body, the Congregational Association, that it was his duty to go to Hanover. His inauguration, March 27, 1822, was well attended. He delivered an address which was set down by the chronicler of the event as " sound, luminous and elegant ", and as a fitting accompaniment to such luminosity, all the college buildings and dwelling-houses were brilliantly lighted that evening.

President Tyler's first days in office were accompanied by the issuing of a new code of college laws, which, printed and distributed, was known as the " Freshman Bible." Even as late as 1822, life was still Spartan at Hanover. Professor Alpheus Crosby, in his " Memorial of College Life ", relates that the hours of study, preceded by one recitation, prayers, and breakfast, began at eight o'clock in summer, and at other seasons at nine, and continued till eleven. Beginning again at two, they held till evening prayers, except Saturday afternoon. Morning prayers consisted of invocation and reading from the Bible; and prayers came daily at five o'clock, or, there being no provision for artificial light in either chapel or recitation-rooms, as early as the president could well see to read in the Bible.

On Sunday the students were required to attend morning and evening prayers in the chapel and two services in the college church. Students were required to be in their rooms during study hours and after nine P. M. and " to abstain from all loud conversation, singing, playing on musical instruments, and from all other noise which may tend to interrupt ", and on the Sabbath every student was " to remain in his chamber unless the duties of public worship or acts of necessity or mercy " called him elsewhere, and no one was to attend to any secular business or diversion, or unnecessarily walk in the fields or streets.

Keeping or playing with cards or dice was punishable with a fine of five dollars, and persistence in either by rustication. Under similar penalties students were forbidden to be present at a " treat " or entertainment in which spirituous or fermented liquors were used. The faculty was " particularly and earnestly recommended to inform themselves concerning each one's moral and literary character ", and to this end was directed to make weekly visits to the room of each student.

At this period it cost the Dartmouth student about one hundred dollars a year for his college life. Tuition was fixed at twenty-six dollars, room rent averaged six dollars, and decent board could be had for one dollar a week; the man who paid one dollar and seventy-five cents was regarded as rather Lucullan in his tastes. To these expenditures were added, according to the individual's moral lapses, the money collected by the faculty in the shape of fines for infraction of the college laws. This species of taxation was no less silly and futile than in other American colleges of the day, but no more so.

Early in the Tyler régime, the requirements for admission were stiffened somewhat. It was now necessary that a prospective freshman be " well versed in the Grammar of the English, Latin and Greek Languages, in Virgil, Cicero's Select Orations, Sallust, the Greek Testament, Dalzel's Collectanea Graeca Minora, Latin and Greek Prosody, Arithmetic, ancient and modern Geography, and that he be able accurately to translate English into Latin."

The college year was of thirty-seven and a half weeks, with three vacations. The seniors were given a special vacation of five weeks after the final " exams ", this " to allow the members to go home, get their new clothes (often homespun) and make other preparations." Their year of study was taken up with Locke, Edwards on the Will, Butler's Analogy, Stewart's " Philosophy ", " Evidences of Christianity ", and " Law and the Federalist " — a sufficiently solemn preparation for the beginning of the duties of life.

In this era the faculty, which for a number of years had comprised only the president, Professors Adams and Shurtleff, and a brace of tutors, was much strengthened by the addition of William Chamberlain as professor of Greek and Latin languages; Charles B. Haddock, a nephew of Daniel Webster, as professor of rhetoric and oratory, and Doctor Daniel Oliver as professor of intellectual and moral philosophy. These were strong men, Haddock in particular, who was one of the most esteemed instructors of his time, and the first professor of rhetoric in America. The fact that he was eternally in debt did not militate against his popularity. It is related that one irate creditor came to Hanover determined to get his money from the professor or proceed to the law. He was royally entertained in Haddock's courtly way, and before he left his debtor's residence, he had loaned the reverend gentleman another goodly sum.

Innovations came thick and fast, as President Tyler's administration waxed. The annual catalogue, long a mere hand-bill published by each sophomore class and bearing only the names of the students, became an octavo pamphlet of fifteen pages, containing the regulations for admission, the curriculum, and the estimate of students' expenses, though it was not published by the college until 1836.

Another change, which must have seemed momentous in those days, was the bricking up of all the ancient fireplaces in the students' rooms of Dartmouth Hall, and the installing of those new-fangled heaters called stoves. Still another was the abandoning of the scheme of compelling the students to fit up their rooms for the holding of recitations. These equipments were primitive and not expensive, but the undergraduates rightly believed that the college ought at least to pay for its class-room furnishings. These were usually a plain table and chair for the instructor, a small blackboard in one corner, a stove, and on either side of the room a double row of long, unpainted, pine benches, hacked and battered with rough usage. Crosby relates that his initial recitation as a freshman was prepared at a table made by piling one trunk on another, and by a light struck from flint and steel. The college now took over a few rooms for regular class-rooms and paid for their fittings, which event was duly celebrated by appreciative verse in one of the New Hampshire newspapers.

In 1825 the college uniform epidemic reached Hanover and laid vigorous hold on the students.

Yale had adopted academic regalia five years before, and Union soon after. So on March 15, 1825, the Dartmouth men voted to adorn themselves after the reigning fashion. Their dress was a single-breasted black frock coat with rolling collar, having on the left breast a sprigged diamond three and a half inches long and three inches wide; and on the left sleeve half a sprigged diamond for freshmen, two halves placed one above the other for sopho-mores, three for juniors and four for seniors; with black or white pantaloons, stockings, vest, and cravats. This outfit, which seems to have been tasteful enough, met with general favor, but soon palled and " survived no longer than the first suit lasted."

A reform more enduringly appreciated ˙was the ukase that the first bell for chapel should never be rung earlier than five o'clock in the morning! This was regarded as considerable of a concession to laziness, but even its clemency was often irksome.

"It was, indeed, barbarous," says Lord, " and the occasion, no doubt, of much injury to health in the more inclement seasons. It gave occasion likewise for many laughable incidents. Attendance was expected at prayers, even though, as sometimes happened for certain classes, no recitation followed. It was not unusual in such cases, and in summer weather, for students to rise from bed at the last moment and, without giving themselves the trouble to dress, to attend to their places, wrapped from shoulder to feet in the long wide cloak then in fashion, ready to return to bed till breakfast. There is an authentic record of one who suffered the misfortune, when thus habited, of becoming involved in a rush, and being pitched headlong down the chapel steps and out of his cloak."

The democracy of Dartmouth, which has been traditional and is still sound, received its first vital test in Tyler's administration. It was not a question of poverty versus wealth, for none, or very few, were wealthy, but a problem of the inclusion of white skins and black in the same college. In the settlement of it, the students showed themselves more liberal than the trustees.

The incident arose over the application of Edward Mitchell, a young man of African blood from the island of Martinique, for admission to the freshman class in 1824. He passed his examinations, but the trustees declined to admit him on the ground that the students might find him objectionable. Whereupon the undergraduates held a mass-meeting, voted that Mitchell ought to be admitted, and appointed a committee to lay their decision before the governing body. The spokesman, C. D. Cleveland, 1827, had an unusually dark skin, and he argued that if a man's color were to keep him out of college, he himself had no business there. The trustees quickly reversed their decision, and Mitchell became a popular member of the class of 1828, graduating with credit. From that day to this, no man has ever been denied entrance to Dartmouth, or, once inside, has been less respected, if worthy of respect, because of his complexion or his race.

After six years of faithful and honorable, if not brilliant service, President Tyler resigned. He had never really loved his work; the call of the pulpit and pastorate was ever strong within him. When he was invited to the Second Congregational Church at Portland, Maine, in May, 1828, the desire to be once more a shepherd of souls exclusively was overmastering. In August, 1828, he left the presidency, carrying with him the respect and liking of students and townspeople for his deep sincerity, his ready sympathy, and his accurate conception of justice. He was not a strong personality, and it appears that the trustees of his day ruled rather rigorously. But results count, and his administration was one of steady advance and increasing common sense.

President Tyler was succeeded by Nathan Lord, a minister at Amherst, New Hampshire, and a Bowdoin man of the class of 1809.

CHAPTER VIII

WITH the coming of Nathan Lord to the presidency of Dartmouth, there was established the physical tie that binds the college of 1828 to the college of to-day. Many of the alumni are still living who sat beneath the mild gleam of his green spectacles, who listened to his pungent remarks on student disorder, who faced his rapier cross-questioning in the pleasant study whither they had been summoned for mental and moral delinquencies. In his long reign of thirty-five years, he so impressed upon his " young gentlemen " — he always called them that, at least — his force of character, his initiative, his self-reliance, his democratic ideas, that it is truly said of him that " probably the distinguishing marks of the Dartmouth type of man were received from him more than from any other source."

When this rural teacher began his work at Hanover, he was the youngest college president in the country, and the youngest man, save one, who had ever been elected as head of an American college.

But at thirty-six he had already given signs of strength. He had been a trustee of Dartmouth for two years, and an aggressive and influential one. He knew what was to be done, and he had perfect confidence that he knew how to do it. He plunged into his labors with enthusiasm and vigor, backed by a harmonious board of trustees and the good-will of the alumni in general.

There was plenty for the young president to begin upon. The college was in its chronic poverty-stricken condition, although there was a little sunlight through the clouds in the form of a partly completed subscription begun under President Tyler, by which, at a meeting of Dartmouth men held in the Exchange Coffee House at Boston, about six thousand dollars had been raised. Thus early the Boston alumni showed that splendid devotion to their college that has marked them ever since, and has made the capital of Massachusetts the capital also of Dartmouth loyalty and endeavor in the eyes of the sons of the institution.

President Lord, having been given the by no means honorary office of financial agent of the trustees, set himself on the money trail with the keenness of a sleuth-hound. It was hoped to raise fifty thousand dollars; but in order to make any subscription binding, a minimum of thirty thousand dollars must be raised. In spite of all Lord's arts of pleading and cajolery, the last day of grace arrived, and only $29,600 had been subscribed. The president, being what might to-day be affectionately termed at Hanover a " dead game sport ", extracted the necessary four hundred dollars from his slender pocketbook, although he had already given three hundred dollars, and saved the day.

With this providential manna, the debt to the John Wheelock estate was paid off, and for the first time in its history the college owed nobody but itself. It was like a boy with some pocket money as a new experience. Dartmouth Hall was remodeled by tearing out rooms in the center and creating " Old Chapel ", familiar to all Dartmouth men now alive down to the class of 1908, and hallowed by the memories of youth rather than by any sanctity of holiness. A new bell and a clock were added to the cupola, and two dozen two-bushel baskets were bought for the salvage of the library, in case of fire. The yard was graded, and around it was placed " a sufficient fence." The college was putting on style.

More important still, the two severe outriders that now flank the new Dartmouth Hall were built and named Wentworth and Thornton respectively, for the generous royal governor and the hearty English squire. They were the first additions to the buildings of the college proper since 1790. The old wooden chapel was hauled away by the combined motive-power of forty yoke of oxen and a score or two of students. Refreshments were, of course, inevitable. The college treasurer had to pay for: " 1 Bbl. cider, 17 soft Buisquet, 20 loaves of Bread, 100 Crackers, 21 lbs. cheese, 6 tumblers, 3 gal. A gin, 3 do. N. Rum, 1½ do molasses ", besides two more quarts of gin and three of rum as extras. There is no evidence that the bill was disputed.

One of the early trials of President Lord was the matter of disciplining his young gentlemen. Whether they had grown a trifle too boisterous under the mild Tyler, or believed that they could impose upon the new " Prexy's " youth, the fact was that there was much disorder after his coming. But the disturbers soon got a taste of Nathan Lord's force. A few ringleaders having been punished, the rest of the students declared a revolution. William H. Duncan, 1830, thus describes what happened: " Some will recollect the electric effect of a speech of Dr. Lord's to the students who were moved to rebel. They had threatened to leave college *en masse* (as they often do if their wishes are not complied with). One sentence from Dr. Lord went like a loaded shell into their ranks. It was this: ' Go,

Hanover Inn

young gentlemen, if you wish; we can bear to see our seats vacated, but not our laws violated.' This was said with such regal decision and dignity that no man of those classes spoke of deserting the college."

However, this was by no means the end of the rough pranks and even outrages that the Dartmouth students of that era seemed to find a berserker joy in committing. Some of these performances were mild, as the seizure by the freshmen of a smoky stove in their recitation-room and the casting of it into the river. Some were excusable, as the tearing down of a house of bad reputation known as the " Seven Nations " and the tarring and feathering of a vile " townie ", who compelled his daughter to dance unclad before some students.

Other exploits were less commendable. It was thought humorous to smash freshmen's windows, sprinkle their rooms with assafoetida, or worse, and break their furniture. To install a flock of turkeys in the chapel, and cows and horses in the upper corridor of Dartmouth Hall, known for generations as " Bed-bug Alley ", was regarded as meritorious, while to conceal a skunk in an instructor's desk against his lifting the lid in the morning was thought a triumph of genius. Wild outbursts of gun-firing were common, to the extent that special laws had to be passed against the inflictions. There were still worse offenses. A vote of the faculty expelling one particularly heinous sinner is illuminating:

Whereas Sophomore Warren appears, from evidence, to have been the leader of a party of students, in disguise, who broke open a citizen's house, threatened the inmates with death, and finally not proving successful in gaining possession of the house, threw large stones through the windows and doors to the manifest danger of the lives of those within; whereas the said Warren is said to have carried a loaded pistol on the night of the above mentioned attack, and whereas the said Warren, though put on strict probation for his misdemeanors, still persisted in a course of dissipation and secret violation of college laws, such as frequent participation in convivial entertainments at a public inn, the keeping of ardent spirits in his room, and feasting upon stolen fowls which students had fattened in the college building and other violations too numerous to mention, therefore voted that Sophomore Warren be and is hereby expelled from college.

Sometimes mere noise took a ponderous and destructive form. A famed incident occurred in the summer of 1836, and is thus embalmed in a letter written home by Solomon Laws, of the class of 1836:

We have had rather squally times here this term. The difficulties arose in and have been chiefly confined to the Sophomore class. They were assembled at a student's room and made some noise, and one of the Tutors went in rather abruptly and imprudently ordered silence &c, when some of them insulted him. For this two were suspended for three months. At this some of the class were much offended, and on the night following some individuals took a large cannon from the gun house in this village, drew it up near the college building about under the offending tutor's window, and fired it with such tremendous charge as to break about three hundred and twenty squares of glass from the college buildings. It jarred the houses in most distant parts of the village, was heard several miles distant and supposed to be an earthquake. The rogues soon returned but the Faculty were on the alert immediately, went to the students' rooms to see whose shoes were wet (for it had rained some) and tried some into the tracks where they drew up and fired the cannon, and found the boots of one to fit some of the tracks. With this and some little other evidence they [sic] faculty expelled him. They could not detect any others.

The members of the faculty, it will be noted, were expected to be and were detectives of no mean rank. Many of them acted as police officers, and they were, from the students' point of view, perniciously active at night, skirmishing about the buildings, sometimes in disguise, listening at doors for signs of forbidden practices. Even President Lord himself was not averse to a merry chase after nocturnal roisterers now and then, and it was told of him by a member of the class of 1846, that in pursuit of said member one night, the honored head of the institution fell sprawling into an open ditch, but retained presence of mind enough to detect the identity of the culprit by his laugh. The president would also mix with a " rush ", and his " Desist, young gentlemen, desist ", accompanied by the pounding of his cane on the ground, was a famous slogan for years.

The concerted blowing of fish-horns enlivened many an otherwise dull Hanover evening. The origin of this custom is lost in obscurity. Lord thinks that perhaps the sound of the conch shell, with which the first president assembled his students, or of the horn, that in his day and again on the failure of the bell in 1820, called the college to its duties, so caught the fancy of the students that they were unwilling to let it pass away. At any rate, faculty legislation was directed against it as early as 1835, and J. W. Barstow, of 1846, says:

" Horn-blowing was in full vogue and blast from 1842 to 1845, but the origin of the vicious habit antedated my own college days. I remember that in 1843–44 the practice had become general in college, so much so that the Faculty had magnified the nuisance into a crime, until at length expulsion was threatened to any student caught with a horn in hand, or even found in his room."

The " Great Awakening " of July, 1851, is traditionally believed to have marked the high tide of

" horning." On the seventh of that month, a hundred or more students had gone to a postponed " Glorious Fourth " celebration at St. Johnsbury, Vermont, to lend Professor Sanborn, who was to give the oration, their moral support. It turned out to be immoral, for bottles of rum were carried along, and the collegians, becoming somewhat uproarious, rebelled at the poor service at the banquet and interrupted the post-prandial speechmakers with cat-calls. A member of Congress, one of the disturbed, wrote violent letters to the press about it, and the faculty had to notice the affair. On the night of the twelfth the students, angered because the case had been taken up for discipline, let loose what the Oldest Inhabitant is wont to call the most hellish three hours' pandemonium of horns, cow-bells, devil's fiddles, and other noise-producers that the town had ever heard. For this eleven men were " separated."

" Horning " survived in milder form a great many years. In the middle eighties it became a testimonial of disapproval for professors or tutors who had offended a class, or an insulting defiance from freshmen to sophomores, who would quite often respond with volleys of stones or coal from the dormitory most frequented by " Sophs." In 1896, the students voluntarily decided to give up the practice. But in 1848 it was still considered necessary by the faculty to pass such a resolution as: "Voted, to require Sophomore Reed to deliver up his trumpet wherewith he discourseth most horrible music to the college and furthermore to apologize to Professor Chase for his insult to him, and in default thereof, to be suspended from examination. N. B: Reed is also to be admonished for blowing his horn, during Professor Brown's recitations."

Such pranks as occasionally marked the activities of Nathan Lord's "young gentlemen" would be considered rather silly business by Dartmouth men of to-day — and silly they would be, for very good reasons, one of which is that there are now so many other things to do. But it must be remembered that in the forties and fifties student effervescence was rigidly corked by faculty and trustee law. Theatricals were banned; cards were rigidly prohibited; dancing was in such bad odor that on one occasion thirty-one students were fined two dollars each for going to a school of instruction in the wicked art; even bowling was frowned upon. The military company called the "Dartmouth Phalanx", by means of which some youthful excess steam had been legitimately let off, was abolished in 1845, because it was deemed too devoted to spirits. Most of the things that were prescribed were dull, while most of the things that were amusing were proscribed.

However, the purchase in 1848 of a fine new eight hundred dollar hand-tub, most appropriately named *Phoenix*, brought much joy and opportunity for useful activity, for in term time the students manned its long pump-sweeps and hose with a will. It was often suspected that old barns and other worthless buildings were set on fire by the boys, in order to furnish the sheer delight of fighting the flames. President Lord used now and then to come out and direct, in his courtly way, the fire company's endeavors. He never forgot his suave and cultivated manner of speech on such occasions. Once, as the youthful firemen were playing upon a burning store on Main Street and directing the stream too constantly at one spot, the president mounted a stone block in front of the Dartmouth Hotel, commanded silence for a moment, and then, sweeping his right arm back and forth in an expressive semi-circle, cried in his clear and penetrating voice: " Gentlemen of the machine — more scope; more scope! " They supplied the scope, and the building was saved.

Doctor Lord's keenness at reading the interior of students' minds was proverbial. " The President with eyes of green ", wrote J. W. Barstow, of '46,

" was Dr. Lord, for he wore the same green specs in my day, and on to the end, worn (it was evident to every student) not so much as a protection from the sun's glare, but as they furnished a secure fence, behind which the dear old Shepherd could glare at his sheep without detection and watch every possible thing that happened to be going on in his vicinity, whether in chapel or recitation room or even in the solemn personal interviews with luckless students in the dreaded 'Prexy's Study.' I have seen him in chapel open the Bible, repeat a psalm (apparently reading it) and his restless eyes meanwhile over the edge of his glasses, searching every face in every seat and every corner. No wonder that he was credited with semi-omniscience."

The death of Daniel Webster in 1852 furnished the most solemn observance of the times at Hanover. The college buildings were draped in black, flags were put at half-staff, college exercises were omitted for a day, and a meeting was held in the chapel, at which it was decided to ask Rufus Choate to deliver a commemorative oration at the next Commencement. That historic address was given in the old church before the most distinguished audience it has ever held, while as many more clamored for admission outside and even tried to storm the doors.

The eulogy is said to have made an extraordinary impression. " For almost two hours and a quarter," says Lord, " Mr. Choate held the dense and eager assembly in almost breathless silence." This Commencement was long in ill favor in other respects, for the hotel men raised their rates to exorbitant figures and, according to one of the New Hampshire papers, there was " an usual amount of fighting, drinking, and general rowdyism in and about certain underground liquor dens, one of which was connected with the principal hotel in the village."

Despite occasional excesses of this kind, more on the part of visitors and " townies " than of students, life in Hanover had been gradually improving. For example, the *Family Visitor* of May 15, 1844, informed the college world that " Mr. Kinsman has constructed a neat and convenient bathing house, which will be open in a few days." The little building stood on the south side of Wheelock Street, nearly opposite the site of the present Episcopal Church. For a number of years it enjoyed considerable patronage. Among others who made use of it were the young ladies of Mrs. Peabody's school, which was kept in a house where Webster Hall now stands, who were required to form a weekly procession thither with soap and towels.[1] The

[1] " History of Dartmouth College," Vol. II.

common was fenced to keep out the villagers' cows. The "Hanover Ornamental Tree Association" was formed, and to its blessed labors the Dartmouth of to-day owes many of its beautiful trees.

The railroad reached the near-by Lebanon in November, 1847, and the old, picturesque, but inconvenient days of the stage-coaches from Concord, from Brattleboro, from Burlington, and from Haverhill, laden with jolly students, their boxes and trunks strapped in mountainous piles behind, were gone forever. There are Dartmouth men still living who recall the coaching days with delight. And they could not have been so very slow. From Boston, the trip to Hanover could be made in a day and a half; it takes practically one day now. Rates were six cents a mile, and there were no rebates for "coach sickness", nor for damage resulting from capsizes, which were not wholly unknown.

Before the advent of the locomotive, the college, under Lord, had begun to crowd the stage-coach tops more and more. There was a rapid growth from 1835 to 1842. From an average of one hundred and fifty students, there was an increase to two hundred in 1836 and to three hundred and forty in 1840. In 1842 there were graduated eighty-five men. Yale that year sent forth one hundred and five, Harvard fifty-five, and Princeton forty-five.

Again Dartmouth had, comparatively, passed the " small college " phase of Webster's plea.

Pressure for room began to be felt seriously. " Bed-bug Alley ", Wentworth, and Thornton were over-populous. A new building was imperative, and the will of Honorable William Reed, of Marblehead, Massachusetts, bequeathing seven thousand dollars at once, ten thousand dollars more after the passing of another of the legatees, and twelve thousand five hundred dollars at the pleasure of the widow, seemed to point a providential way. The old Wheelock mansion, southwest of Thornton, was moved away (to become the Howe Library of the present day) and on the site, Reed Hall was built, — a plain structure, but of beautiful proportions and destined in later years to be considered a place of residence for Sybarites, because it was long the only dormitory heated by steam.

In 1842 came a sudden shock to the pleasant plans for a growing college. Due mainly to the financial distress of the country just before that time, the entering class numbered only forty-three and graduated but thirty. In 1845 there were but one hundred and seventy-nine academic students in the whole college, as against three hundred and forty-one in 1840. A sorry hole was made in the receipts from tuition, while expenses ran on as usual. To make a bad matter worse, the Reed legacy hung fire, and Reed Hall had to be paid for.

There was but one thing to do: start another subscription; and Nathan Lord went at that thing with his characteristic energy. The sum of fifty thousand dollars was asked for, on the condition that thirty thousand dollars be raised before August 1, 1843. The effort failed, and would have died utterly but for the generosity of Samuel Appleton, of Boston, who refused to take back his thousand-dollar check and advised another subscription. This was attempted, with another time limit set at August 1, 1845. Again the amount lacked completion, this time by four thousand dollars, and again rare old "Sam" Appleton came forward with a check, giving nine thousand dollars, and raising himself to deserved canonization in the annals of Dartmouth.

A few years later came a bequest that proved more easily collectible than that of William Reed. This was of fifty thousand dollars from Abiel Chandler, of Walpole, New Hampshire, for "the establishment and support of a permanent department or school of instruction in the practical and useful arts of life." With this money was founded the Chandler Scientific School, afterward called the Chandler Scientific Department, and in 1893 completely merged with the college.

NATHAN LORD

In the Lord era, the Dartmouth students, as those of other colleges, took their politics pretty seriously. In 1856 a Republican Club was organized, and an amusing account is preserved of a debate in the chapel between Edward F. Noyes, later a Union general and governor of Ohio, and the Democratic postmaster of Hanover, Reverend Daniel F. Richardson. The club raised a splendid 120-foot flagpole in the middle of the campus, made by two Maine students who had previously been shipwrights. This pole lasted till 1869, though its political origin was often overlooked for the more attractive fact that its crosstree furnished an admirable display-point for utensils and figures that the students deemed proper for exposition.

Scales, in his history of the class of 1863, relates that on one occasion the effigy of a New Hampshire judge, who had made himself obnoxious to the students, was thus suspended from the pole. An investigation followed, in which a student was asked if he had any part in raising to the crosstree the man who had there fixed the effigy, and he promptly replied: " I did not," and was dismissed. After graduation, he met Professor Aiken, and, recalling the circumstance, asked him if he remembered his reply. " Yes," said Professor Aiken, " but I always felt that you were not telling the truth."

" I did," he replied, " for I was the man who was pulled up." Another man, noted for his untidy person and slovenly dress, on being called before the faculty, admitted that he was disguised. On being questioned as to the nature of his disguise, he hesitated and stammeringly said: " Well — I — I — had on a clean shirt."

The epoch of Nathan Lord was necessarily one of change, experiment, and development. Much can and does happen to any college in thirty-five years. Several of the innovations pleased the president's " young gentlemen " greatly. They liked the abolition of college honors and the giving of Commencement parts to everybody, though the faithful audiences of parents, friends, and sweethearts must have suffered torments when, as sometimes happened, they had to sit through the forensic efforts of fifty " Commencers." This terror was afterward abated by the adoption of a system of drawing lots for Commencement parts, a scheme President Lord stubbornly refused to change, even against the almost unanimous request of the faculty and an appeal from the Boston alumni. His answer was that honors were " unchristian and immoral as making an appeal to wrong motives and hurtful ambition." The trustees stood by him in this view of the matter. To the students it seemed a great gospel of peace.

Equally popular was the final extinction of the chapel exercise in the dawn and its removal to the after-breakfast hour, though the young gentlemen were a bit saddened by the rearrangement of the chapel seats, by which it was made impossible for the sophomores to " rush " the freshmen out through the doors and down the granite steps. But again came compensation: the evening prayers were abolished in 1860; only a few of the old New Hampshire Puritans were known to take this as evidence that Satan's black wings were spreading over the Hanover plain.

The question of slavery, that touched many another American college in the middle of the nineteenth century, came to Dartmouth with peculiar intimacy and finally forced its great president into retirement. Nathan Lord in his earlier days had been a stout abolitionist. His conversion to proslavery was almost as sudden and startling as was Paul's to Christianity. In 1847 he read a pamphlet by one B. F. French, of Lowell, arguing that the bondage of the black man was divinely ordained. From that moment he appears to have believed likewise. He wrote public letters, using all his arts of logic to persuade the world that slavery was defensible, " not as it existed in this country or as it ever existed anywhere on the whole ", but *per se*, apart from its abuses, as an institution of God according to natural and revealed religion, that, like war or pestilence, was designed by God as a penalty for sin; and he called it a divine institution, not because it was blessed, but because he believed that it was divinely ordered.[1]

This was a bit too subtle for the average Northern conscience, and although the president was kindly disposed toward the negro, actually helping fugitive slaves from his private purse and admitting colored students refused from other New England colleges, his peculiar views aroused great hostility toward the man and toward the college itself. In the college no one was particularly disturbed; the students excused the president's opinions on slave-holding as one with his " peculiarities."

With the coming of the Civil War, however, this peculiarity became the centering-point of violent attacks, natural enough under the changed circumstances. The good old doctor was accused of being a traitor, whose words were giving aid and comfort to the enemy. One of his letters to the *Boston Courier* (November 22, 1862) was reprinted, in garbled form, by the Connecticut Democrats as a campaign document, which did not improve the situation. The president published this as a pam-

[1] " History of Dartmouth College," Vol. II.

phlet in which he held that the true responsibility for the great conflict was upon abolition, as an attempt to subvert the moral government of God. This was the last straw. The church of the North was up in arms at once. Resolutions were passed by the Merrimack County Conference of Congregationalists calling upon the trustees to inquire whether the interests of the college did not demand a change in the presidency.

The trustees could no longer blink the ugly situation. When they met on July 21, 1863, the storm lowered. A motion being made to confer the degree of Doctor of Laws upon Abraham Lincoln alone, that year, President Lord voted against it, making a tie. His foes in the board then presented the Merrimack County resolutions. The majority refused to endorse them; they would not ask the resignation of Doctor Lord, but they went on record as declaring that they did not " coincide with the President of the College in the views which he has published, touching slavery and the war ", also hoping that " American slavery with all its sin and shame . . . may find its merited doom in the consequence of the war which it has evoked."

Upon hearing this, stout old Nathan Lord seized his cane, walked out of the trustee-room, and returned in half an hour with his letter of resignation.

He would quit before he would trim, though quitting took away his livelihood. He could not agree to any "test" of opinion, and also he would not "submit to any censure, nor consent to any conditions such as are implied in the aforesaid action of the board." He held also that it was "inconsistent with Christian charity and propriety to carry on my administration, while holding and expressing opinions injurious, as they imagine, to the interests of the College, and offensive to that party which they here professedly represent."

Such a resignation, tendered in such a style, admitted of nothing but acceptance, and the trustees at once did the obvious thing, doubtless much relieved that the stalwart old fighter, who regarded his convictions as more valuable than his position, had taken a great burden from their shoulders.

Nathan Lord in the retirement of his study — he lived out the remaining seven years of his life in Hanover — could justly reflect that he had done a man's work in his long presidency. He found the college groping; he left it walking erect and firmly. The faculty had increased from ten to seventeen. The shabby old college buildings and unkempt grounds had been transformed, and three new halls and an observatory had been erected. The assets of the institution had grown from eighty-five thousand dollars to two hundred and one thousand dollars. And the president had sent 2,675 young citizens into the world, most of whom were doing something that the world wanted done.

To-day Nathan Lord's belief in the divine origin of slavery becomes trivial. What he did for Dartmouth and the essential Dartmouth man is not forgotten.

CHAPTER IX

DARTMOUTH COLLEGE gave 652 of her sons to the service of the military forces that kept the Union whole. Some were old men; most were in their early vigor, and some again were mere boys who, when they had fought out the fight, returned to college or came for the first time. Classes were represented from 1822 to 1884. With these 652, Dartmouth furnished a larger proportional number of soldiers for the Civil War than did any other college of the North. On every battlefield, in every hospital, in every camp, on the march and in the bivouac, the men of Dartmouth were to be found doing their duty, dying bravely or living honorably as the god of battle decreed.

Dartmouth has as yet no noble hall for a Valhalla to her soldier heroes; but she has two bronze tablets in "Webster", and she has a little green book with the Great Seal stamped in gold on its cover. This book is the "Dartmouth Roll of Honor", and within its 137 pages is enfolded the story of the devotion of one New England college to its government and its flag.

In this memorial we find that 204 men were commissioned as surgeons or assistant surgeons, thirty as second lieutenants, forty-seven as first lieutenants, sixty-seven as captains, sixteen as majors, twenty-one as lieutenant-colonels, twenty-four as colonels, and four as brigadier-generals, and some of these received additional honors "for meritorious conduct" in special engagements or for the war, three having the brevet rank of captain, one of major, three of lieutenant-colonel, nine of brigadier-general and three of major-general.

When the news of the firing upon Sumter reached Hanover, the few students from the South, whom President Lord's pro-slavery views had attracted to Dartmouth, went home in a hurry. A military company of sophomores was immediately formed and called the "Dartmouth Zouaves." It was well drilled, but performed no actual service. On May 8, Charles Lee Douglas, of the class of '62, enlisted in the First New Hampshire, and, it is believed, was the first college undergraduate to join the Union Army. Others dropped out of college from time to time, but it was not until May, 1862, that any general exodus of student-warriors was threatened. What then happened caused the faculty some anxiety. A high-spirited, brilliant young junior, Sanford S. Burr, of Foxboro, Massachusetts, a magnificent horseman, " talked war day and night " and induced a hundred students to promise to organize with him a company of cavalry. New Hampshire, Maine, and Massachusetts declined to accept the troop, but Rhode Island agreed to stand sponsor for it, if it could be raised immediately.

The students were greatly excited; Mars was the only classical hero worth mention. President and faculty advised the young men to stick to their books, but made no attempt to coerce them. Finally only thirty-five men left Dartmouth, and other institutions were drawn upon to make up the eighty-five known as " The College Cavaliers." These youthful horse reached Washington, June 30. On the way, " elegant handkerchiefs and fans were forced upon the acceptance of the students " by Philadelphia ladies. It must have needed force, indeed, to impose " elegant fans " on Dartmouth cavalrymen.

The squadron did good service at Harper's Ferry, and in September captured a supply train of eighty-five of Longstreet's wagons. It was mustered out in October, and most of the Dartmouth men returned to Hanover, where they were piqued to find that, patriotism or no patriotism, they would have to pass the examinations that had been held during their military pilgrimage. They threatened to secede to Brown in a body, whereupon the Dartmouth faculty promptly surrendered to the youthful veterans, who all resumed their places in the college.

It was not only those fired by young blood who entered the service of their country. Many men far past the military age limit, mostly, of course, as surgeons and chaplains, joined army or navy. The oldest of whom there is record was Henry Wood, of the class of 1822, who was sixty-five when the war broke out. He was a chaplain in the United States Navy, but not a war recruit, for he had served since 1856. Ebenezer Hunt, 1822 (Medical), was sixty-four when commissioned assistant surgeon of the Eighth Massachusetts Volunteers. Nathaniel Gould Ladd, another surgeon, had reached sixty-three at the time of his brief, but honorable service.

One of the noted Dartmouth "Medics" who ministered to the wounded, and himself died of illness incurred in the line of duty, was Luther V. Bell, of the class of 1826. Doctor Bell was commissioned surgeon of the Eleventh Massachusetts on June 13, 1861. In September, so splendid had been his work, he was appointed brigade surgeon of

Hooker's Brigade, and then promoted to be medical director of Hooker's division. The horrors of war impressed him at once. Following the first great disaster at Bull Run he wrote to a friend:

The whole volume of military surgery was opened before me on Sunday afternoon (July 21, 1861) with illustrations horrid and sanguinary. Sudley Church with its hundred wounded victims will form a picture in my sick dreams so long as I live. I have never spent one night out of camp since I came into it, and a bed and myself have been strangers, practically, for months; yet I have never had one beginning of a regret at my decision to devote what may be left of life and ability to the great cause. I have, as you know, four young motherless children. Painful as it is to leave such a charge, I have forced myself into reconciliation by the reflection that the great issue under the stern arbitrament of arms is, whether or not our children are to have a country.

Stirring was the career of Rufus Gilpatrick, of the medical class of 1834. Going to Kansas in 1854, he plunged with all his soul into the wild turmoil that surrounded the making of that territory into a free State. He became an intimate and ardent friend of John Brown and with that noble fanatic engineered the " underground railway " for the escape of fugitive slaves. He was a leader in the fiery politics of the period; was president of the first State Congressional Convention and presidential elector in 1850. When the war broke out, he became surgeon of a brigade organized by General James H. Lane. His service with the Army of the Frontier was notable, both as a field surgeon and as secret agent of the United States. At the battle of Webber's Falls, in the Indian Territory, he bravely remained behind his command, to minister to a wounded soldier, and was shot dead, while in this act of mercy, by a company of Confederate soldiers.

To these Dartmouth men and to the two hundred more who, either as surgeons or assistant surgeons, gave the best there was in them to their allotted work, the country owes loving remembrance.

Dartmouth's army chaplains were many and of honorable fame. Perhaps the best known to the men of the college, because of his long service as Latin professor, was Henry Elijah Parker, the beloved "Picker" of later days in the classroom. He was commissioned chaplain of the Second New Hampshire in June, 1861. Chaplain Parker was closely and continually associated with the regiment all of the time of his service. The men of the regiment always had a very friendly and kindly feeling for him. He was in the battles of First Bull Run and Williamsburg, and others in which the regiment was engaged. He always succored the wounded without heeding whether he was under fire or not.

A militant man of God was Daniel Foster, '41, chaplain of the Thirty-third Massachusetts. At Chancellorsville, seizing a musket from a fellow soldier, he rushed into the ranks as a self-made recruit. From that time on he was, of course, known as the " fighting chaplain ", and in November, 1863, was transferred to the Thirty-seventh United States Colored Volunteers, with the rank of captain. Like so many other officers, he led his dusky troops with great bravery, fighting at the Wilderness, Spottsylvania, North Anna, Cold Harbor, and the siege of Petersburg. Like so many others, too, he mingled his life's blood with that of the negro, being killed at the head of his regiment at Chapin's Farm, September 30, 1864.

Another alumnus who was not too proud to cast his lot with colored troops was Royal Parkinson, '42, chaplain of the Twenty-third United States Regiment, which was one of the first to enter Richmond. He was not content with preaching and praying, but taught the men arithmetic, geography, and history in quieter times in camp.

Alonzo Hall Quint, '46, of the Second Massachusetts, was one of the famous chaplains of the war.

His bravery in action, his devotion to the men, his wide and tender sympathies, made him a notable figure in any division in which the Second was included. It is related of him that after a great battle he found one of his regiment dying upon the field. He knew that the man was a Catholic. Breaking a couple of twigs from a bush, he tied them in the form of a cross and held the emblem before the soldier's fast glazing eyes. " The smile of joy upon the poor fellow's face ", said the chaplain long afterward, " assured me that I had performed something of the work of the Master, and I was glad." Parton, the historian, called Mr. Quint " one of the bravest chaplains of the war ", and Colonel Cogswell's report to the Second Massachusetts, said of him: " It is not improper to speak of this officer as having always (and especially in time of action) been of the greatest value to the regiment. His energy and perseverance were of the highest order." Chaplain Quint wrote letters from the field to the *Congregationalist* during his three years of service, and after the war published a history of his regiment. He was one of the organizers of the Grand Army of the Republic, and suggested the motto on the badge of the order.

Another noted figure who wore the insignia of a chaplain was John Eaton, '54, for many years after the war United States Commissioner of Education. Beginning as chaplain of the Twenty-seventh Ohio, he ended his service as colonel of the Sixty-third United States colored Infantry, and retired with the brevet rank of brigadier-general. In the intervening years his career was varied and exciting. Twice he was a prisoner within the Confederate lines, once being requisitioned to preach to the enemy's soldiers. In 1862 he was appointed by Grant superintendent of the negroes, who in multitudes were pilgrims into the great commander's lines in Alabama, Tennessee, and Mississippi. He proved a marvelous organizer of the black folk's efforts to be of use.

George Webb Dodge, '50, was one of the few army chaplains who knew the bitterness and horror of long captivity in Confederate prisons. He was commissioned, April 20, 1861 — one of the very first chaplains to join the army after Sumter — in the Eleventh New York Volunteers, the famous Ellsworth's Zouaves. At Alexandria he climbed the fatal stairs of the Marshall House with his colonel to help haul down the rebel flag, and stood beside him when the enraged innkeeper fired the shot that was to keep Ellsworth's memory bright forever. At the first battle of Bull Run, Chaplain Dodge was taken prisoner. Then began a weary year of shifting from one prison to another. At first came Libby, not so very appalling at that early day; then Castle Pinckney, South Carolina, where the chaplain nearly died from yellow fever; then Charleston jail; then the dreadful Salisbury, North Carolina, with its miasma, its stenches, its boiling sun, and its human cruelties; then Libby again, now filthy, vermin-haunted, and heart-breaking. But the chaplain preached and prayed and cheered his comrades until he was exchanged in July, 1862. The twelvemonth, however, had done its work, and with broken health he resigned from the army.

Arthur Little, '60, was the youngest of the Dartmouth chaplains of whom there is record. He was twenty-seven when commissioned in the Eleventh Vermont in March, 1863. He saw the horrors of the Wilderness and Cold Harbor and was active in caring for the wounded. At Charleston, Virginia, a classmate, Colonel George E. Chamberlain, was mortally wounded and died in his arms. In that gallant soldier's unfinished letter to his wife were these words: "We are in God's hands; and his will is better than our will; we will love him and trust him and be satisfied." He also saw his brother-in-law, Captain E. B. Frost, '58, expire of a terrible wound, received at Cold Harbor, "happy to die for my country and for my God." Chaplain Little's magnetic preaching was long remembered by the men who went through the dreary winter before Petersburg.

On nearly every great battlefield a Confederate bullet struck a Dartmouth heart. Some of the killed were but lads, who had left the college for the camp. A splendid type of these young patriots was Dennis Duhigg, who would have graduated in 1863, but enlisted in the Fifteenth Vermont in September, 1862, as a private. In two months he was promoted to sergeant-major for gallantry. He became first lieutenant of the Eleventh Vermont and was made a captain just before the battle of Winchester. In that engagement, when the order came to charge the enemy, he shouted as he took his place: " Come on, boys; I have never driven you, but I will lead you." In a few moments he fell, mortally wounded. " My last prayer is offered. I die happy," he murmured, as he was " mustered out."

Arthur Edwin Hutchins, '57, first lieutenant in the Eleventh New Hampshire, fought with conspicuous gallantry at Fredericksburg in the McClellan campaign and before Vicksburg. At the battle of the Wilderness, serving on the staff of Brigadier-General Griffin, he was given an order to carry to another commander. " Make all speed ", was his instruction, " for on your celerity depend the lives of ten thousand men." Spurring his horse, he dashed across an open field, unmasking the enemy's position as he rode. " But ", says the " Roll of Honor " with simple eloquence, " neither horse nor rider ever stirred again."

Oliver Tucker Cushman, '63, enlisted in his junior year in the First Vermont Cavalry. From sergeant to second lieutenant, to first lieutenant, to captain, he made his way. Terribly wounded in the face while charging with General Farnsworth at Gettysburg, he returned to Hanover, but could not rest content. He rejoined his regiment in October and then, its term of enlistment having expired, he re-enlisted and kept on fighting. His hour of fate came at Hawes' Shop near Richmond, June 3, 1864, just as he was about to receive his commission as major. Of him said General William Wells: " He was not only one of our bravest, but also one of our best men, and had he lived would have obtained a high rank in the army. His company was devotedly attached to him, and his superiors in command, as well as all his associates, bear witness to his high character as a soldier and a man."

Another undergraduate who earned his special place in the " Roll of Honor " was Richard Bailey Crandall, '63, who left college in the autumn of

1861 as adjutant of the Sixth Vermont. In less than a year he was its major. To an extraordinary degree the joy of battle was for him a high emotion. "To have lived a minute then was worth a thousand years", he said of the gallant but fruitless charge up the heights of Fredericksburg. The college and the army were the poorer when a Confederate bullet ended his life during the gigantic sharpshooters' contest along the entrenchments at Cold Harbor.

Some men of the great conflict preferred death, or the risk of it, to the torture of Libby, or Andersonville, or Salisbury prisons. William Carter Tracy, '58, was of that stamp. As first lieutenant in the Fourth Vermont, he was in every battle fought by the Army of the Potomac from McClellan's ill-starred peninsula campaign to the awful slaughter of the Wilderness. Twice wounded in that titanic struggle, he refused to leave the head of his company. Recovering, he was with his regiment on June 23, 1864, when it was placed in the Weldon railroad near Petersburg. All at once Confederates sprang up before them as if some magician of war had tapped the earth. The Vermonters were outnumbered five to one. Only the line of railroad iron toward the Union lines was open. "Surrender", yelled an officer of the "Johnnies." Most of the regiment threw down their arms. "Cut for it", shouted Lieutenant Tracy, running down the track. A few of his men followed him; but so did a Confederate bullet, passing through his head.

William Lawrence Baker, a Chandler Department man of '58, was a dashing lieutenant of artillery in the Fourth United States. At Winchester, though but comparatively new to the service, "his bearing was that of a veteran." Sighting and firing his guns himself, he cut to pieces an attack intended to capture his battery. For his heroic conduct here and at Port Republic he won warm official praise. He deserved better of fate than to die alone, with no man to take a farewell message from his lips. When the awful field of Antietam was searched, after the conflict there, Lieutenant Baker was found lying by one of his guns. A smile was on his face, though a bullet had pierced his heart.

Dartmouth was compelled to claim one deserter. Yet his name is included in the " Roll of Honor ", and rightly. Franklin James Burnham, '69, rose from a private to first lieutenant in the Ninth New Hampshire, and saw South Mountain, Antietam, Fredericksburg, Vicksburg, Jackson, Wilderness, Spottsylvania, Cold Harbor, and Petersburg on the way. In the Mississippi swamps chills and fever nearly finished him. After recovery in a Kentucky hospital, he was sent to the Veteran Reserve Corps, an honorable enough but totally stagnant assignment. It did not suit at all this Dartmouth man, who had been a brilliant leader in college activities. He deliberately deserted and, with some difficulty and some privations, made his lonely way to his regiment and reported for duty to his astounded superiors. He received promotion instead of a court-martial, and there is a tradition that Lincoln sent him a quaint and characteristic letter, endorsing that kind of a deserter and wishing there were more like him in the army.

Thus could the little green book be drawn upon for story added to story of the valor and devotion and faith of the men of Dartmouth in the four years' appeal to arms. Those who survived flowed back to their homes in a great tide of usefulness. Empty sleeves and crutches became but the commonplaces of a new life in the community. The embedded bullet could not stop a career. In the halls of Congress; in the capitols of States; in the classrooms of great universities; in famous pulpits; in powerful banks; in vast manufactories; in foreign legations; in pioneering on the seven seas, the Dartmouth veterans made themselves felt, and many of them are still, fifty years after " Appomattox and its famous apple-tree ", virile and active in every line of human endeavor.

THE "DARTMOUTH ROLL OF HONOR"

For those who did not survive, it is one of Dartmouth's great hopes that soon it will be true, in deed as well as in word, that

> The granite of New Hampshire
> Keeps the record of their fame.

CHAPTER X

WITHIN three weeks of the day when Nathan Lord stamped out of the trustee room and the presidency, a new head of Dartmouth College had been chosen, and within two months more he had been inaugurated in a raging storm and to the harrowing music of a neighboring village's " Cornet Band." As late as 1863, rural simplicity governed inaugurations at Hanover. In fact, " pomp and circumstance " never did appear at such events until the installation of Ernest Fox Nichols in 1909, when the college had ceased to be " small " and had acquired sophistication.

The new president was Reverend Asa Dodge Smith, D. D., of the class of 1830, the distinguished pastor of the Fourteenth Street Presbyterian Church, New York. There was for some time to be no change in the custom of choosing a president from the clergy, a custom previously broken only in the case of John Wheelock. Doctor Smith was distinctly urban in style, in manner, and in looks, though one might, perhaps, have rated his infantile,

North Massachusetts Hall

cherubic face as a little more indicative of guileless-
ness than was the fact. He was of fine height and
bearing, and he always appeared in public in a well-
tailored dress coat, immaculate shirt front adorned
by two large gold studs, and a high collar of the
stock variety, about which was wound the finest
black satin cravat that money could buy. Doctor
Smith, it will be understood, brought a whiff of
metropolitan air to the country college, and it was
undoubtedly a beneficial element. The first genu-
inely city man to occupy the president's chair at
Dartmouth, he gave to it a certain distinction that
proved very useful later on.

No sooner was President Smith fairly seated than
some of Nathan Lord's policies were either badly
maimed or killed outright. But if it hurt the retired old warrior to see the slaughter, he gave no
sign, even when his cherished scheme of assigning
Commencement parts by lot was abolished and
scholarship again made the test, or when prizes,
considered by him as immoral, were instituted, and
prize speaking contests at Commencement between
juniors and sophomores were revived.

The ancient Quarter Days, occasions of vast out-
pourings of oratory, debates, poems, and music,
were also resurrected in a vain attempt to restore
the former vitality to the old societies, the United

Fraternity and the Social Friends, which had now become mere custodians of libraries and divisions of the students in general football exercise on the campus. The " Junior Exhibition " was established in the spring term, orations being expected from fifteen or more men on the basis of their scholastic ranking.

For a while the new order aroused genuine interest, but it soon became irksome, and the exhibitions went out of existence. The last to die was that of the juniors, which survived until 1878. For several years these exercises were made the butt of a mock programme gotten out by the sophomores in a style sometimes witty and always more or less scurrilous. As a composite of several efforts, with the worst features omitted and family names changed, the following may be submitted:

LOGICAL DISQUISITION

" Some pumpkins are green;
I am green;
Therefore, I am some pumpkins."
G-assy W-indbag Howard.

———

ORATION

" How I made the spondoolix fly — or
My twenty-five cent bust.
Little Charlie Birrell.

THE FIRST CITY PRESIDENT

ETHICAL ORATION

" Aint I a hard boy? "
F-oolish W-itless Jaynes.

Before this *promising* youth concludes his happy effort the audience will be fully convinced that in his case " truth is stranger than fiction."

SCIENTIFIC DISSERTATION

The Darwinian theory reversed, or the monkey descended from (a) man.
A-wful L-ibel Rumsey.

TIGHT ROPE PERFORMANCE

W-ild A-pe Lloyd.
C-lass M-onkey Cray.

Lloyd doing the tight and Cray the rope.

SYRIAC ORATION

" Zlpoknxquevwatvpolecat."
J-ackass S. Converse.

MUSIC

" Hark from the tombs a doleful sound."
To be sung by the audience.

During the exercises W-illing C-atspaw Woodside, the class fag, will circulate a slop-pail for the convenience of those sick at the stomach.

With demoniac howls the class repair for the denoue-
ment to Bed Bug Bar Room, where they close the exercises of the day with a

GRAND FINE ALE.

While it was never confessed, the probability is
that the " Junior Exhibitions " were abandoned by
the faculty for the sake of putting an end to the
accompanying outbreaks of Rabelaisian humor.
The " Social " and " Fraters " divisions of the
whole college went on in a perfunctory fashion, most
men neither knowing nor caring to which society
they had been assigned by the faculty, until June,
1904, when the traditional fragments of the organizations voted to give up their respective ghosts and
convey their libraries to the college.

No college president is without a money problem;
none ever can be. President Smith met his with
supreme tact and energy. It was not for nothing
that he had come from a rich congregation and was
well known in New York. When he passed the
academic hat in that town, goodly checks fluttered
into it. The trustees encouraged him to set a one
hundred thousand dollar goal as the limit of his
money-raising endeavors. Within three years, thirty
thousand dollars was obtained, and the president
further secured during his administration additions

of seventy thousand dollars to the scholarship funds of the college.

Some reasonably handsome bequests came along in Doctor Smith's time, among them one of one hundred thousand dollars from Judge Richard Fletcher, of Boston, ten thousand dollars of which was reserved as a fund for a biennial prize for an essay " to counteract the worldly influences that draw professed Christians into fatal conformity to the world ", which ponderous theme proved so unattractive a magnet that it was afterward deemed advisable to ask the courts to permit some other use of the money. Judge Joel Parker, of Cambridge, left one hundred and forty thousand dollars for the benefit of a library and for the purpose of founding a law school. This also was impracticable, and the fund was used to establish a professorship of law and political science. Another bequest, a splendid gift, of a quarter of a million dollars, came from Tappan Wentworth, of Lowell, with instructions that it be allowed to accumulate until it had reached half a million.[1] The gifts to all departments of the college during Doctor Smith's administration amounted to $960,590.

But much of this money was not immediately

---

[1] In 1896 this fund reached the desired mark and the income began to be of use to the college.

available, and straitened financial conditions went on as usual. The trustees had begun to realize that the faculty was miserably underpaid. A full professor got only eleven hundred dollars and the president eighteen hundred dollars. In 1865, these sums were increased to thirteen hundred dollars and two thousand dollars; in 1866 to fifteen hundred dollars and two thousand dollars, and in 1869 to two thousand dollars and three thousand dollars, at which notches they stuck persistently for a score of years more.

The students were made to assist in this laudable work to some degree. The annual tuition fee was raised from fifty-one dollars to sixty dollars in 1867; to seventy dollars in 1872, and to ninety dollars in 1876. The "graduation fee", politely supposed to be expended for diploma costs, was set at eight dollars, and it is there yet.

Happily, the chronic poverty of a college never makes it misanthropic or morose. When 1869 reached the scene, it found that great preparation had been made for a joyous Centennial celebration at Dartmouth. This was held on Wednesday of Commencement week. Realizing that the church could not hold a quarter of the people who would come to Hanover, and the hotels not a tenth part, a huge tent, two hundred and five feet long and eighty-five feet wide, with a seating capacity of five thousand, was borrowed from Yale. This was set up at the western side of the Common, while over on the eastern edge was erected a great board barracks, three hundred feet long and forty feet wide, for a dining-hall. A photograph of the Common thus decorated shows that the college grounds must have looked as if a cross between a " Greatest Show on Earth " and a military encampment were in progress, the latter resemblance being increased by the presence of two good-sized tents, where Rollins Chapel now stands, for the classes of 1867 and 1868, and a hundred army wall tents back of Dartmouth, used as bachelor quarters for the general alumni.

The food for this occasion is said to have been historically bad, though furnished by an able hotel man, Asa T. Barron. "There was, perhaps inevitably ", says Doctor W. T. Smith in his " Hanover Forty Years Ago ", " considerable complaint in regard to the catering in general and the dinner in particular, so that when, after Commencement, Mr. Barron invited several members of the faculty to take a trip among the mountains as his guests, a local wit, Ira B. Allen, remarked that he did this ' to take the cuss off the dinner.' "

The morning exercises went very well. There

was a procession, and as it passed the house of ex-President Lord, hundreds of his " young gentlemen " of other days uncovered, as the face of the veteran was seen at his chamber window. Salmon P. Chase, then Chief Justice of the United States and President of the Alumni, was master of ceremonies in the tent. Suave President Smith made a speech of welcome " in his happiest vein ", and there was a historical address by President Brown, of Hamilton College, son of Dartmouth's third president.

But in the afternoon there came an unbidden guest who made things very disagreeable for the festal throng under canvas. He did not register, but it was proven beyond doubt that his name was J. Pluvius. He had rarely been in better form.

Professor John K. Lord, who was present on that direful afternoon, gives us a lively picture of what happened. " Judge Chase ", he says, " began the exercises with a pleasing extempore address. Three of the assigned addresses were then given, when, to break the succession, a poem written for the occasion by George Kent of the class of 1814 was read by Judge Barrett of Vermont. As he was reading, there came the interruption for which there had been no provision. A shower, announced by heavy thunder, burst upon the tent as if the very windows of heaven had been opened, and the audience made the appalling discovery that the tent was not waterproof. Judge Barrett, who was of stuff too stern to yield to wind and rain, held his post and only read the louder. But it was of no use; at first in vapory thinness, then in sheets and streams, the water poured through the canvas of the tent. A few had umbrellas, some held settees as a roof above their heads, others, including the Chief Justice and most of the dignitaries from the stage, sought beneath the platform a refuge from the flood, but they had forgotten the cracks between the boards, and as the water poured through them in concentrated fury, the disappointed victims found that their last estate was wetter than their first.

" The shower was as brief as it was fierce, and as it passed away, the audience took heart with the returning sun and though clothes were soaked, toilettes disarranged and finery ruined, it resumed its place with numbers almost undiminished. Judge Barrett who had left the stage with slouched hat and dripping garments came back and finished reading the poem. Senator Patterson delivered his address, which Mr. Duncan says ' was by no means a dry one,' and received the compliment of ' the undivided attention of the audience which had been thrown into confusion by the storm, and which was not only wet, but soaked and thoroughly uncomfortable.' "

The bedraggled orators and auditors could stand no more, and the rest of the speech-making was put over until the following afternoon. But the students obligingly gave their naive gymnastic exercises in front of the tent, to the great delectation of the crowd, which, in that archaic era, had not learned the fiercer joys of the Commencement base-ball contests. Could the Dartmouth students of to-day be induced to perform in a body with staves, dumb-bells, and Indian clubs for the delight of the admiring friends of Class Day Week? Could those of any college, for that matter?

After the Commencement feast in the long shed next day, the " main top " was again crowded. Governor Stearns assured the college of the State's distinguished consideration, though he did not promise any money. General William T. Sherman, who had been given the LL. D. degree in 1866, made a neat speech after the inevitable and, to him, finally dreadful " Marching Through Georgia " from the Boston band in attendance. Great joy was afforded by " Long John " Wentworth, the famous millionaire pioneer of Chicago, who remarked, apropos the professions of great embarrassment on the part of several who had preceded him: " Perhaps you think I'm embarrassed, but I ain't." This, as he deliberately hoisted his colossal bulk of six feet and ten inches above the heads of the audience and glowered about him, nearly brought down the tent. An evening promenade concert under the huge canvas, overpoweringly illuminated by the glare of half a dozen locomotive headlights, brought the Centennial festivities to a brilliant close.

The life of the Dartmouth undergraduate in "Prexy" Smith's day was simple. For many, teaching in the winter months was a regular routine, and all over northern New England the boys and girls of the "Little Red Schoolhouse" felt the influence of Dartmouth training, which often included thrashing the boys and making love to the girls. A long vacation of six weeks just after Thanksgiving made matters fairly easy for the young pedagogues. Even after changing the terms and shortening the winter recess, the custom continued in a measure and was not unknown in the late eighties.

Returning teachers brought back with them the money which enabled them to meet their college expenses and also experiences that were both valuable and interesting. Most of them taught in schools where "boarding round" was the regular practice, and the teacher went from family to family, according to a definite system determined by the number of children going to school. As each family usually delayed the annual killing of the pig till the coming of the teacher, his customary meat diet through the term was fresh pork and sausage. It was no uncommon thing for a student to break his own road through the snowdrifts to the schoolhouse and to build the fires. The conditions of his work were primitive, and the subjects which he taught were not advanced, but he widened his acquaintance, learned adaptation and self-dependence, and brought back to college the confidence born of success.[1]

The *Aegis* for July, 1861, contains a statement as to the students engaged in teaching during the year 1860–1861, from which it appears that out of the 275 members of college, excluding the students of the Medical and the newly-organized Chandler Schools, 173 taught during the year. The aggregate length of their schools was 2,278 weeks; the total amount earned was $23,089.75, and the total net amount brought back to college, after deducting payments for board and other expenses, was $14,-185.75, a sum that would have paid the expenses of all who taught, for tuition, board, room-rent, fuel, lights, and washing, reckoned at the maximum rate of $174.50 given in the catalogue of that year. At

[1] "History of Dartmouth College," Vol. II.

the minimum rate of $124.50, the proportion of expenses met would have been much larger. Of the 173 who taught, there were thirty-five seniors out of a class of fifty-seven, forty juniors out of sixty-five, fifty-two sophomores out of seventy-two, and thirty-seven freshmen out of eighty-one. Of the schools sixty-four were in Massachusetts, seventy-six in New Hampshire, twenty-five in Vermont, and three in Maine.

Slowly came liberalizing in rule and event for the students of this era. A reading-room was opened on the ground floor of Dartmouth Hall, the trustees contributing forty dollars a year for its upkeep, and the undergraduates contributing the money for papers and magazines. The library, which had hitherto been a chaos of poorly catalogued and generally unobtainable books, was made respectably workable and attractive. The college church, known to its reluctant Sabbath devotees as the " barn ", was painted and had its seats widened and provided with cushions, " so that one could go to sleep upon them without danger of falling off." Money for this work of mercy was raised by the entertainments in the Dartmouth Hotel, where charades, wax-works, and imitations formed the staple of amusement. In 1872 the afternoon church service was abolished, and a brief chapel exercise took its place, " as a police regulation " to discourage afternoon pilgrimages from town.

The building of the Bissell Gymnasium in 1866 gave a new point for undergraduate interest. This structure, considered something of a marvel in its day, the best in the country, was made possible through the gift of George H. Bissell, of 1845, a New York lawyer. It was ninety feet long and forty-seven wide, was well equipped and actually contained bowling alleys, which had been anathema in the college but a few years previous. Militarism also took its place as an outlet for temperamental exuberance, and two companies, " A " and " B ", of the " Dartmouth Cadets of New Hampshire " were formed in 1873, with uniforms and muskets furnished by the State. These academic militia-men were known as the " Dartmouth Belligerents " and for a time they were impressive.

" Three days in the week ", said the *Dartmouth*, " at a certain hour the two companies of Dartmouth Cadets may be seen parading on the common or in the park. They make a fine display in their neat uniforms of blue, and the instruction in the tactics progresses rapidly." A later issue announced that: " The Cadets, who have attained wonderful pro-ficiency in military evolutions, are also obliged to suspend operations and go into winter quarters."

"Not all were equally alert", says Lord, "and one man marched so lazily that Professor Young, who was one day watching the drill, exclaimed: 'He ought to have a bee in the seat of his trousers.'" In a year or two the "Belligerents" tired of their toys and the companies perished of inertia.

The relations between sophomores and freshmen had not, in President Smith's time, reached their present state of urbanity. "Rushes" of strenuous character were frequent. Chapel seats were daubed with grease, or paint, or molasses. The climax of such performances was reached when the body of Evans, a murderer, was stolen from the Medical School and placed on one of the freshmen benches, past which the sophomores solemnly filed, as the organist played a particularly gloomy dirge. Individual hazing was not unknown, and there is a tradition that one especially obnoxious "fresh" freshman was boxed in a packing-case, which was set upon the rear platform of the southern night express, with the result that the unhappy individual's plight was not discovered until the train was far down in Connecticut. Against such practices the faculty thundered and demanded pledges of abstention, but not very successfully. Time, with its civilizing influences and its changed notions of class amenities, was required for the complete reform. Occasionally, however, the majesty of the law stepped in, as when nine undergraduates were arrested for cleaning out the store of an unpopular bookseller named Parker and were haled to the Plymouth court, by which they were eventually fined $350.

President Smith resigned on December 22, 1877, by reason of ill health, and finally retired on March 1, 1878. During his thirteen years' tenure, the college advanced steadily. The faculty increased in numbers from seventeen to twenty-nine, and the student body reached its largest figure up to that time. Under him the Agricultural College and the Thayer School of Civil Engineering were established, three new buildings were erected, the elective system was begun — " in a limited and cautious use ", as the trustees half-affrightedly put it — but still begun. A system of alumni nominations for trustees was inaugurated, thus paving the way for that intimate relation between Dartmouth men and the government of their college which is excelled in the case of no other institution.

CHAPTER XI

THE MAN OF IRON

THE successor to President Smith was Reverend Samuel Colcord Bartlett, D. D., of the class of 1836. At the time of his election in January, 1877, he was one of the leading professors in the Chicago Theological Seminary, orthodox to the core. Had the trustees searched the world for a more absolute opposite to Doctor Smith, they could not have found the man. Short in stature, swift in motion, incisive in speech, imperious in will, brilliant in intellect, courageous in convictions, he presented a contrast to his urbane, tactful, pacific predecessor that was soon to startle the little college world to which he came.

Had the slang been invented in his day, Doctor Bartlett would doubtless have been called a " live wire." He was charged with the electricity of personality that attracted some and repelled others. At times it was unpleasant to handle him without insulation. But his dearest enemy would not have accused him of lacking brains or force, and few to-day would deny that he believed in Dartmouth, as he believed in himself, and was sincerely devoted to her interests as he saw them.

In the mellowing process of the years, the controversy that raged about him is now seen to have been of much less importance in principle than it seemed to the spectators of the drama in the " eighties." It was a thunder-storm that cleared the air, dispelled the perfervid heat, and brought the rainbow of promise for the immediate years to come. But it naturally seemed very tragic while it lasted.

The mutterings preliminary to the tempest began to be heard soon after President Bartlett entered upon his term of office. Curiously enough, the small and then comparatively unimportant scientific school, founded with old Abiel Chandler's fifty thousand dollars in 1851, was the storm-cloud. President Bartlett, a severe classicist, was temperamentally incapable of feeling any liking for this department. He believed that it was living beyond its means, that it was getting too " hifalutin " in its curriculum and that it was " sapping " the college by hiring the latter's instructors for extra work at small pay. He was doubtless jealous of its fine appearance on paper, for, with the names of the special instructors from the college added to its own, the list in the annual catalogue was more imposing than that of the college itself.

Promptly the new president took action. He had the members of the academic faculty withdrawn from their " extras " in the Chandler School — they received two dollars an hour for the work — and a long and bitter contest was instituted as to the Chandler curriculum. The men of the latter institution arose in arms at once; they thought the president was set upon degrading them and their school. The college faculty was split into two camps, one — by far the larger — disliking Doctor Bartlett for his uncompromising style and his peremptory way of cutting off their means of increasing their slender earnings, the other intensely loyal to him because of that magnetism that attracted some of his support.

Bitter speeches, unjust charges, fiery literature, and pungent pictures soon made Hanover a somewhat too exciting seat for a college. Naturally, the students were uneasy, fractious and ill-behaved. For the *Aegis*, the junior illustrated annual, the class of '84 obtained the services of *Puck's* greatest artist and printed a full-page colored cartoon of a dog-fight, with President Bartlett as the central figure, flanked by one or two faculty supporters, frightfully mauling his adversaries and being bitten by them in turn. It was characteristic of the president, who had a sardonic brand of humor, that he was not at all outraged by this masterpiece, privately declaring that he could not complain very much, since he was depicted as the winning dog, *par excellence*.

Naturally, the trustees were distressed at this quarrel, which was fast outgrowing the bounds of the college. But, though they employed their ablest and most generally successful pacificator, Reverend Alonzo H. Quint, D. D., to try and bring peace to the hostiles, they were for some time unsuccessful.

The alumni now began to assail the president violently, and on April 7, 1881, the association at New York voted to ask the trustees to investigate the civil warfare. On April 29, sixteen of the twenty-three resident members of the faculty signed a paper demanding Doctor Bartlett's resignation. They declined, however, to make any specific charges against him, although given opportunity by the trustees. The New York alumni were not so circumspect. They formulated, in a style that is now seen to have been coarse and needlessly insulting, the following accusations:

First. That said Bartlett by his habitually insolent, discourteous and dictatorial manner in official intercourse with his associate members of the Faculty has stifled all free and independent discussion of college matters and that he has illegally ignored and usurped the functions of the Faculties of various departments of the College.

Second. That said Bartlett has deliberately and intentionally imperiled the influence of the Faculty with the students and has improperly endeavored to bring certain members into disgrace in the eyes of the students and the public.

Third. That said Bartlett has persistently and systematically exerted his official influence to impair and diminish the prosperity of the different Departments of the College.

Fourth. That in his public official relations to the students said Bartlett has used such language as to necessarily humiliate and disgrace them and graduate them as enemies instead of friends of the College.

Fifth. That said Bartlett has so far lost the confidence of his associate members of the Faculty that out of a total membership of twenty-three residents sixteen openly express the belief that the best interests of the College require his resignation.

The president's trial — for it was almost that in character, and was conducted against him by Judge William Fullerton, of New York, for the alumni, in the manner of a case against a common pickpocket, until the eminent criminal lawyer was savagely rebuked by the great New Hampshire barrister, Harry Bingham, for the president — was held in Hanover on June 17 and on July 12. Doctor Bartlett won decisively. " While the charges ", said the committee in its report to the trustees, " were serious, the specifications were inadequate, many of them trivial, nearly half of them were withdrawn, and as a whole unsupported by adequate proof of any important error. . . . The committee do not think that the formal investigation has disclosed any results which sustain, so far as acts and words go, a claim that there should be a change of office."

At this rebuff, fifteen hostiles of the faculty tendered their resignations. The trustees refused to accept them. There was no secession. Still the outside world believed that the president was under pressure from the trustees to retire, so that in April, 1882, the latter thought it wise to announce the following:

To put at rest the disquieting rumors that have been circulated, to the effect that the Trustees desire the resignation of President Bartlett,

Resolved. That we put on record the expression of our continued confidence in him as an able, efficient administrator, and an admirable instructor and we believe that the best interests of the College require that he should continue in his present position.

Resolved. That we believe that the best interests of the College require that the members of the Faculty should continue in their present positions and cordially co-operate in advancing the true interests of the College.

The acute stage of the quarrel gradually passed away, and the stalwart old president ruled with

The Tower

more modified power for ten years longer. In spite of the battle against him, in spite of his unpopularity at the time of the fiercest tilts, his administration was fruitful. He obtained the gift of a new chapel from Edward Ashton Rollins, of Philadelphia, and was instrumental in raising considerable money for new professorships. The Wilson Library was built during his reign, and to his genius for rugged effect is due the fine stone tower at the top of Observatory Hill, to the building of which students from '85 to '95 actually contributed a deal of back-breaking toil. He was prime mover in the improvement of the enchanting park near by, convincing the undergraduates that labor donated to road and path making on Wednesday and Saturday half-holidays would be amply repaid in the days to come — as it has been. He devised the method of moving the sixty thousand books of the library from their perilous quarters in Reed Hall to the new building — a long procession of hand-barrows with a student at the end of each one, by means of which the entire literary load was transferred in four days, every man in college having a finger in the business.

As has been observed, "Prexy" Bartlett had a caustic wit. Some sophomores once conceived and put into execution the brilliant coup of installing a donkey at his desk just before some exercises in "Old

Chapel." Upon ascending the steps of the platform and finding the visitor tied to his chair, the president was expected to show some confusion. But confusion and he were never intimate. Piercing the rows of " Sophs " with his penetrating glance, he observed icily: " Young gentlemen, when you have removed your brother from the platform, the exercises will proceed."

Such a man was naturally his own dean, proctor, and private detective. He believed in the *argumentum ad hominem* that consisted of mingling valiantly in a " rush " and extracting men from the same by their coat collars. He was an intimate president, who had the habit of occasionally materializing in a student's room to catch him in some particularly obnoxious devilry. A man of iron in an iron age. A man who fitted absolutely the academic landscape of his time. It was he who began the early foundations of the new Dartmouth, and though his faults of temperament and style be admitted, the fair-minded of to-day recognize the value of his work.

Looking backward, it is clear to see that the Dartmouth student of these roaring " eighties " imbibed something of the rugged nature of his environment. He was a more self-assertive gentleman than is his descendant and champion of college honor to-day.

THE MAN OF IRON

He realized, by some subtle instinct, that he was the ultimate product of the fast disappearing Iron Age of Hanover. His swagger was more genuine, his contempt for the niceties of the sartorial science more profound and consistent. An ulster, concealing who may now say what lack of apparel under its garishly sheltering folds, was not merely a help to morning devotions — it also typified a superb indifference to small conventions in the way of dress. A celluloid collar was not only an embodied economy — it was also a shining defiance to laundries, their uses and abuses.

Whether this inherent opposition to the finer things of life was a disadvantage, or not, it is difficult to say. We now know that it was but temporary, and most Dartmouth men of that period are so satisfied to have been a part of those glorious days that not for the great gift of another youth would they lose their memories to become merged in the golden epoch of the present Dartmouth. And they like to think that the iron has not passed away, but that it still stands, a firm and imperishable basis for the ornamentation of the gold.

It is curious to note that in this seemingly unpromising epoch blossomed a literary garden such as had not been previously known in the College. More men began to write, and write better, than ever before. Some of their work was, naturally, imitative; some was strongly original; but all of it was an honest and refreshing departure from the ponderous, pseudo-classical bombast of preceding years.

Several elements, apart from the natural bent of men who happened to come to Dartmouth at that time, were responsible for this awakening. The influence of Arthur Sherburne Hardy, then professor of mathematics, who had just leaped into fame with his " But Yet A Woman ", was potent. The inspiring work of the lamented Charles F. Richardson, professor of English literature, was becoming more and more fruitful. The *Dartmouth Literary Monthly* came into being and furnished a sympathetic outlet for the product of aspiring authors. The whole atmosphere seemed suddenly charged with the impulse to write.

Perhaps the genius of Richard Hovey, who wove his spell about the ancient halls and the more ancient hills and dales of Hanover in the early " eighties ", was the most powerful incentive to serious literary attempts by many of his confreres. His personality had an amazing appeal. The writer of this " Story " thus set down his recollections of the poet as a student for the *Dartmouth Magazine* of June, 1905: —

" It was on a beautiful and balmy evening in

early September on the campus of Dartmouth College that I first knew I saw Richard Hovey. I say ' knew ' because, as I look back upon those days of romance and the flush of youth, it seems to me that it must have been impossible not to have noticed in the old chapel or out under the elms that sturdy figure and that dark and handsome face that no man could look at and pass unheeding by. I must have been attracted by the great, liquid eyes; the black, curling beard, common enough with young collegians in the roaring ' eighties ', and the magnificent, leonine head set on the shoulders in the manner of a piece of classic statuary. Spite of my Freshman woes, my settled conviction that I had sunk lower than ever mortal man had sunk before, I am sure that the wonderful personality of Richard Hovey must have been a part of my picture of the new and academic world.

" But on the evening of which I speak my impressions of Hovey were positive and never to be effaced. The dreadful Sophomores had, a little after supper, gathered on the big green and were shouting coarse and unmannerly invitations to us, the still unswaddled class of '87, to come forth with our rubber football. We came, we saw, we — fought. By no means a doughty warrior myself, I was at last flung off the periphery of the struggling human wheel and deposited not over-gently on the turf. As I paused for a moment to reconnoitre, I heard in a most melodious and eloquent voice this adjuration:

" ' Up, boy, and at them! '

" Such a command, a sort of cross between the genial request of old Horace for more Falernian and the order of a French marshal to his troops, was interesting. The man who made it was more so. To my young fancy he seemed Alcibiades turned cowboy. He wore a dark blue flannel shirt, fastened at the neck with a great, black bow, and his remarkably handsome head and face were set off by a grey felt hat with a flaring, bandit-like brim. Tweed trousers were tucked into long riding boots, immaculately polished. Surely the ' groves of the academy ', as President Lord used to delight to call Dartmouth, had never seen such a figure before, I thought. But I was wrong. They had seen Richard Hovey for two years, and he was now a Junior, urging uninspired Freshmen into the fray.

" We soon came to know that Hovey was a man like no other. He was eccentric, bizarre perhaps, but he stood for the beginning of the literary renaissance at Dartmouth, that was to make the period from '83 to '93, approximately, somewhat noteworthy in the history of the College. As he became in after years by far the greatest poet that

THE MAN OF IRON

Dartmouth has produced, so was he in his Hanover days by far the most essentially poetic and fascinating personality that ever dreamed away the spring-time under the old trees. There were those who believed him mildly insane; sage townsmen, from behind the safe ramparts of their prosaic counters, would tap their foreheads after he had left their stores with a jest they could not understand and a bit of the blossoming of a thought that must have seemed to them miles away in the skies. Afterward they came to know the truth and were, to a man, proud of their acquaintance with 'Sir Richard.'

"The College love that always thrilled the warm heart and the great brain of the man was a notable emotion of his student days. First of all, I think, came the beauty of the region that encircles our Dartmouth. Four years of intimate acquaintance with the hills and valleys, the forests and ledges roundabout implanted within him a passionate affection that never cooled. He was an inveterate wanderer, and his wooing of nature did not always please that jealous mistress, the College corporate. But in the end it did more to reflect glory upon Dartmouth than anything of perfection he could have attained in any of his classrooms."

In the Bartlett period, the long-continued pressure from the alumni for genuine representation in the board of trustees came to a focus and won a great victory. The sons of the college were dissatisfied with the compromise of 1876 by which the trustees had agreed that the next three vacancies in the board were to be filled by alumni nomination, and that from the first four names certified by the alumni the trustees " ordinarily and, in all probability, invariably " would elect a man. This plan did not provide for continued and intimate representation, as the three were elected for life. The alumni insisted upon short terms for men elected absolutely by their own votes.

There was some notion of obtaining an increase in the number of trustees by act of legislature, but the spectre of the great " Case " was still too discouraging for that experiment, since the charter said in English that could hardly be mistaken: " The whole number of said Trustees consisting and hereafter forever to consist of Twelve and no more." An act enlarging the board to seventeen members was, indeed, passed, but conditioned on its acceptance by the trustees, which was never voted.

After a lively campaign of debates, addresses, resolutions, and letters, the alumni at the Commencement of 1891 came to an agreement with the trustees by which they were empowered to nominate " a suitable person " for each of the five trusteeships next becoming vacant and the successors to those offices. Thus there have ever since been five alumni trustees in the board, each holding his place for five years (usually re-elected) and one resigning each year. The plan has worked with the smoothness of fine machinery; the personnel of the board has been broadened and strengthened, and the interest and loyalty of the sons of Dartmouth have been enormously increased. Feeling that they are helping to run their own college, the alumni have tided the institution over many a crisis, giving generously of time, money, and moral support.

In February, 1892, President Bartlett resigned. He was no longer under fire, and he wanted to do " certain special literary work." The trustees, in agreeing to his retirement, paid tribute to " his unsurpassed energy in administration, his untiring and incessant labors, and his undoubted love and devotion to the College." " During his presidency ", they said, " the tone and standard of scholarship has been raised; the range and choice of studies has been broadened and extended. The number of professors in the College and various departments has been increased from twenty-one to thirty-four; new college buildings have been erected;

the library has been enlarged from 54,000 to 72,000 volumes; and the friends of the College have contributed to its funds — including that given for lands and buildings — over $700,000; and during this period all the funds of the College have been scrupulously kept to the purposes for which they were given."

The alert, sinewy figure of the rugged old man was familiar in Hanover for six years more. Often it was mounted on a bicycle, which the ex-president rode gallantly and well up to his eightieth year. Occasionally it was seen in the lecture-room, where the keen intellect, unclouded always, revelled in presenting to the students its orthodox conceptions of the relation of the Bible to science and history. Even in the mellower sunshine of the New Dartmouth this strong character was found fighting to the end with the ancient sword of Gideon for a faith that was wearing away.

CHAPTER XII

THE GREAT AWAKENING

THERE have been three "Great Awakenings" having to do with Dartmouth College. The first, pre-natal, but with strong influence upon the academic child, was the "Great Awakening" that George Whitefield's revivalistic fireworks brought to the arousing of men's consciences in the New England colonies of the middle of the eighteenth century. In this work Whitefield and Eleazar Wheelock came together; without it Occom and Whitaker might never have been sent to England, and certainly could not so successfully have reached the seats and pockets of the mighty, had they gone at all.

The "Great Awakening" of July, 1851, already referred to as the most dreadful concatenation of ear-piercing and nerve-racking sounds from instruments of torture ever known in Hanover, was a manifestation of youthful wrath at what was conceived to be faculty tyranny, and is worth this paragraph only because of the grim jocosity of its significant name.

The third "Great Awakening" for the college was the administration of President Tucker. It came without pomp of declaration, without sound of trumpets, without hint of fire and sword. But in and out of the college, men soon knew that it had arrived.

* * * * *

When President Bartlett gave the trustees the opportunity of saying complimentary things about him — and with sincerity — he also gave them the way, as it seemed, to name the one who was even then most in Dartmouth men's hearts as he who should come to the succession. Reverend William Jewett Tucker, '61, had been a wise, far-seeing, brilliant trustee since 1878. He had won fame as a sound, forceful, fascinating preacher. He, too, was urban, as all the presidents since Nathan Lord have now been. As professor of sacred rhetoric at the Andover Theological Seminary, he was leading the fight on the famous old "Hill" for the "Andover movement", finding time also to establish Andover House, now South End House, one of the early social settlements in the city of Boston. The charm of his personality, the prophetic quality of his wisdom, and the intensity of his interest in and knowledge of Dartmouth made him the candidate, not only of logic but of sentiment, for the presidency. He was elected with complete unanimity.

But he was unwilling to leave his Andover brother knights in the heat of their tourney against mediaevalism, and he declined. So did Reverend Francis Brown, of Union Theological Seminary, grandson of Dartmouth's third president. For the interim until a permanent head of the college should be found, Professor John K. Lord was made acting-president. He administered the office with marked ability and tact for the complete college year ensuing.

During this period of seeking a president, the Tucker feeling, rebuffed by the very man who embodied it, grew constantly stronger and at last overwhelmed the genuine reluctance of the commanding figure at Andover to yield to it. Trustees, faculty, alumni, and friends of the college everywhere urged upon Doctor Tucker what they believed was his path of duty. A less well-poised man would have had his head turned by this universal demand; one of less visioning intellect would have feared that so much sunshine was ominous of some later storm. It takes a peculiarly strong man to enter upon a new career and do it justice amid the salvos of universal acclaim. If there is any flaw in his armor, the average man tightens it, if thrusts are expected, but he leaves it unmended when all is serene. Doctor Tucker never made this mistake; he throve under good-will, but by constantly striving to be more worthy of it, not content to bask in its genial comfort, as he might have done indefinitely, so uncommon was the power of his personality.

It was but a little while after the inauguration of President Tucker, which was happily on June 28, 1893, that the "Great Awakening" began. Immediately, as if by some widespread instinct that a new force was about to transform the college, the size of the entering classes increased. Freshmen outbulked and out-cheered sophomores in quick succession. In 1893 the sheepskin-takers numbered sixty-nine. In September of the same year one hundred and twenty men entered college. In four years the senior output was ninety-three men, and in ten years one hundred and thirty-five. Students poured into Hanover in a fashion that amazed the ancients and put the trustees at their wits' end to find lodgments for the newcomers. Dormitories were a prime necessity, and, as the president and trustees were set against any private exploitation of dwelling-places for students, with power to conduct them taken out of their hands, the college had to build them. This it began to do, not as a philanthropy but as a business-like investment of funds in hand — a policy that has continued to govern and has proven highly satisfactory.

As a preliminary step, the old dormitories, which in 1893 could accommodate about two hundred students in excessively Spartan fashion, were made a little more habitable. A magnificent water supply system, by which water was brought from a little artificial lake high among the hills to the east, put the archaic pumps out of commission [1] and made bathrooms and running water possible in the buildings. Then came the remodelling of " Bully " Sanborn's house, giving rooms to fifty, and soon after that of Doctor Dixie Crosby, providing for fifty-five more.

Still the increasing numbers hammered at the gates. Richardson Hall, the pioneer of the fine modern dormitories, was the answer, and again fifty-five students were given quarters. Not enough. Then followed, about yearly, the Fayerweather Row, back of Dartmouth, giving rooms for eighty-five; Wheeler, beautifully situated a little north of the chapel, accommodating ninety-eight; Hubbard, holding forty-eight; Massachusetts, with quarters

---

[1] These appliances probably had their own advantages. A Dartmouth man who afterward did great things as an amateur oarsman always maintained that his devotion to water and the necessity of getting it from the campus pump for four years was responsible for his muscular development.

for eighty-eight, and New Hampshire, housing one hundred and seven.

Thus in fourteen years sprang up fourteen dormitories, mostly of handsome brick construction and adding to the capacity of Dartmouth places for seven hundred students. In all this extraordinary development, the seer-like wisdom of President Tucker showed unmistakably. He advised — and the trustees unhesitatingly decreed — that even in the finest dormitories small and inexpensive rooms should be interspersed with luxurious suites, so that rich and poor should be forever housed together. Dartmouth has no "Gold Coast"; she never will have one. She furnishes fine quarters for fine birds, if they care to pay for them, but she insists that their next door neighbors be of plainer feather. For kindred reasons, classes are not permitted to hold any particular dormitories *en masse*.

Another pleasant adjunct to democracy, though it is said to have lost something of its centralizing power of late, was College Hall, built at a cost of one hundred and twenty thousand dollars in 1900. This was, and still is, the house of the college commons, and in the fine, oak-raftered dining-hall some four hundred students stow away their provender two or three times daily with more or less speed and with perhaps more than less of the traditional and

College Hall

inevitable grumbling at college fare. *A la carte* now rules, after unsatisfactory trials of a fixed price per week and of a mingling of both systems. In the basement a " grill " caters to the more irregular eaters and thrives on some men's indisposition to quit their beds in time for the commons' breakfast.

A huge room in this building was fitted up in club style, while the broad, bricked veranda in front, dominating the most conspicuous corner in Hanover, was immediately made popular as an out-of-door " lounge." It has parted with much of this distinction by reason of the great increase in well-equipped fraternity houses of late; but it is still a valuable asset to the college and to the men in it.

A few troublesome legacies came down from the Bartlett era to engage President Tucker. One was the prime *casus belli* of the preceding administration, the relation of the Chandler School to the college. Instead of warring with the school, President Tucker simply had it absorbed by the college itself, and all cause for rivalry and hard feeling at once disappeared. The two faculties were united, and the student body henceforth appeared as one.

Another question to be settled was the kind of financial policy that should be pursued. The college was heavily in debt when President Tucker arrived and was clearly drifting, financially. Doctor

Tucker remade it in that respect. Gifts and bequests he did not despise — magnificent ones were made during his administration, largely because of him — but he held that the business side of the college must be modern and effective.

"Reconstruction with a view to expansion" was the president's idea of the making of the new Dartmouth. He held that in no better way could the funds of the college be invested than in the things the college needed. From that principle arose the great dormitories, the splendid water-supply system; an enormous central heating plant that sends steam through nearly two miles of underground pipes to all the buildings around the campus, in the park, and to the gymnasium; an electric-lighting plant that illuminates all the buildings, and a comprehensive sewerage system that takes the place of the ancient unsanitary and dangerous appliances that can be spoken of, even now, only in whispers. All these things cost money, but as they also saved money, they were productive investments. Some of them actually brought in a profit revenue. When President Tucker wanted a thing, the wherewithal to get that thing was always forthcoming.

The spirit of the alumni toward this extraordinary administration was one of admirable loyalty and generosity. More than once was the latter quality tested. In the midst of a campaign for funds to build Webster Hall, the stately auditorium in memory of " Black Dan ", the telegraph at Hanover village flashed the sorrowful news that Old Dartmouth Hall, the one link to antiquity, the whole " College " for so many years, was on fire and going to its destruction.

Before the venerable and loved building was consumed, President Tucker had called a meeting of the trustees to deal with the problem of its loss; as the sacred ashes still glowed, Melvin O. Adams, the trustee living in Boston, sent to every son of Dartmouth in his region a card upon which was the now historic: " This is not an invitation, but a summons ", calling for a meeting that same morning in Lorimer Hall, Tremont Temple. Four hundred alumni crowded the place on this brief notice, and, with a mighty shout, resolved that Dartmouth Hall must be replaced immediately. At once a subscription was started; the corner-stone of the new building was laid in October, and the completed hall was dedicated on February 17, 1906. In the two years two hundred and fifty thousand dollars had been given by Dartmouth men of all grades of financial ability, and this sum paid for Webster Hall also.

Once more the alumni gave that most convincing evidence of their interest in the college — the pocketbook proof. For a long time the Bissell Gymnasium had been but a poor apology for a " gym ", the deserved butt of sarcasm from Hanoverians and the outside philistines alike. It was seen that Dartmouth, with all its growth, could not take her place in many branches of athletics, handicapped by such a travesty of an indoor plant. From Professor John W. Bowler, physical director and trainer, came the suggestion that the " Men of Dartmouth " be asked to give a new " gym." A committee of alumni went to work with characteristic Dartmouth vigor, and in 1909 work was begun on what is at this time the largest and finest gymnasium in the world, built at a cost of one hundred and ninety thousand dollars.

Some handsome individual gifts also made this fruitful era of " The Great Awakening " still more notable. Doctor Ralph Butterfield, '39, of Kansas City, left one hundred and forty-one thousand dollars to the college, most of which was spent in erecting Butterfield Hall as a museum of natural history, archaeology and ethnology. In 1897 Mr. C. T. Wilder, of Olcott, Vermont, gave one hundred and nine thousand dollars, which resulted in the physical laboratory named Wilder Hall. Later this gentleman gave seventy-five thousand dollars more. The Fayerweather bequest resulted, after long litigation, in $223,381 for the college.

THE GREAT AWAKENING

The largest benefactions of this, or of all times, for Dartmouth, came from Edward Tuck, of the class of 1862, a millionaire banker long resident in Paris. In 1899 he told President Tucker that he wished to establish some memorial of his father, Amos Tuck, '35, and that he had securities then worth some three hundred thousand dollars with him as a foundation. In making this gift Mr. Tuck told Doctor Tucker that it was " my expectation that the present and future Trustees will apply a portion of the income to the increase of existing salaries whenever the best interests of the College demand it, and a portion of the salaries of additional professorships which may in the future be established in the College proper or in post-graduate departments, should such be added at any time to the regular college course."

In a few years the securities so grew in value that they were worth half a million dollars. Professors' salaries were increased by two hundred dollars and some money was spent on the library, but still the greater part of the income was unexpended. In the year of the gift, President Tucker formulated a plan for a graduate school of preparation for the careers of business, banking, and foreign commerce. This he would call the Amos Tuck School of Administration and Finance. He sent details of the proposition to Paris and asked Mr. Tuck's permission for this use of the fund. So delighted was the banker that he employed the cable to carry back to Hanover his swift " amen." A little later he gave one hundred and thirty-five thousand dollars for a building as the home of the institution. Thus arose the Tuck School, first of its kind among the American colleges and remarkably successful in fitting men for life outside the ancient professions. What it purposes to do in its two-year course is thus officially set forth:

The Tuck School aims to meet both the increasing demand of business men for more efficient service and the increasing demand of young men about to enter business for training that will enable them to realize more rapid advancement. It aims to accomplish this by making it possible for young men to begin business careers with the advantages that accompany a disciplined and well-informed mind, a general knowledge of business conditions and methods, and a special knowledge of certain branches of business which have become specialized.

The School does not presume to create the genius for business; it aims in this respect to assist the young man to discover for himself and combine into an effective working force such elements of business ability as he may possess. It does not presume to make of its students men of mature business judgment; in this respect it aims to equip its graduates with those powers of analysis and interpretation necessary to the development of sound judgment in business experience. It does not presume

Tuck Hall

to create experts in any particular line of business; it does aim, however, for many branches of business, to acquaint its students with those rudiments of expert knowledge familiarity with which makes the further acquisition of expert knowledge relatively easy.

The School does not expend its energy teaching those details of business which can be learned most quickly and effectively in later experience; it is the purpose, however, to develop for the business world an exceptional grade of raw material possessing the ability to recognize the significance of routine details in their relation to the organization and administration of a business institution.

But Mr. Tuck's munificence did not stop at that point. In 1910 he gave five hundred thousand dollars more to the college, the income to be used for the laudable and much-needed purpose of increasing the salaries of the faculty. He has recently supplied the money for the building of the beautiful new road through the glens and woods of the Hitchcock estate to a point near the old wooden bridge over the Connecticut. He has given to other needs as occasion has arisen, so that his total contributions to the advancement of his college have been more than one million two hundred thousand dollars.

Another gift of large importance in this golden era was the beautiful and commodious administration building, Parkhurst Hall, presented by Lewis Parkhurst, '78, and Mrs. Parkhurst as a memorial to their son, Wilder Lewis Parkhurst, who died at the beginning of his sophomore year in Dartmouth. In this fine structure are rooms for the president and the trustees, and offices for the treasurer, the business director, the dean, the registrar, the medical director, the superintendent of buildings, and the auditor. A rear extension provides a most artistic faculty room in mediaeval, raftered style and with opposing rows of benches that suggest a small parliament and that would have been used, no doubt, as government and opposition seats, had it existed in President Bartlett's time. Such forensic tilts as now occur there are warranted sound and kind.

Two festal occasions in Doctor Tucker's time brought the " old Grads " back to Hanover in unusual numbers and in especially jovial mood. The first, in September, 1901, was the centennial of the graduation of Daniel Webster, at which time, the corner-stone of Webster Hall was laid by Lewis Addison Armistead, of Boston, a great-grandson of the statesman. In the college church a remarkably penetrating and thoughtful oration was delivered by Samuel W. McCall, '74, of Massachusetts, and at the formal banquet which closed the celebration and opened the new dining-hall in " College ", after-dinner speeches were made by such masters in the art as Edward Webster Sanborn, Doctor Francis Brown, Judge David Cross — even then venerable, but as high-spirited as a colt — William Everett, Edward Everett Hale, Senator George Frisbie Hoar, and Chief-Justice Melville W. Fuller.

But the part of this anniversary in which everybody took most delight was the pictorial, the night parade of September 24. Among the great elms, the largest of which were banded: "We were here with Dan", marched a picturesque procession, headed by a group of alumni horsemen of more or less certain seat. Then followed in order the faculty in black gowns and mortar-board caps; the students in caps and gowns of white, blue, scarlet, and yellow, according to classes; then the large body of alumni, every man togged out in a blue dress-coat, buff waistcoat, stock, dicky, and Websterian tall hat. There were floats bearing Webster's carriage, his large Marshfield plow, a reproduction of his room showing his old hat, chair, and table, and a miniature facsimile of the first college building. Up and down the ranks howled a band of students dressed as Indians. The college buildings were ablaze with electric lights, not so common for exterior decoration then as now. And if groups of "Grads" concluded the festivities later on with mild alcoholic accessories, it was not so very inappropriate to the occasion, and there were no excesses, as there would have been, as a matter of course, a generation before.

By far the most interesting of all Dartmouth's special occasions was the celebration incident to the laying of the corner-stone of the new Dartmouth Hall in October, 1904. For this event the college was peculiarly fortunate, as a matter of sentiment, in the presence of the Earl of Dartmouth, sixth of the title and great-great-grandson of the nobleman who befriended Samson Occom and Nathaniel Whitaker to such financial advantage in 1766. The Earl, the Countess and their daughter, Lady Dorothy Legge, were given a reception by the students that astonished and delighted them. The old "Wah-Hoo-Wah" cheer was roared forth for their delectation upon every possible occasion, with or without excuse. Their keen amusement at this essentially American bit of academic enthusiasm was apparent.

On the night of the first day a series of tableaux illustrating various events in the history of the college was given on a large stage before the grandstand of Alumni Oval. Here again sentiment was admirably wedded to art, for the Samson Occom of the living pictures was Charles A. Eastman, the Indian alumnus of 1887. The scenes in detail were:

THE GREAT AWAKENING

(1) Wheelock receiving Samson Occom at Lebanon, Connecticut, December 6, 1743; (2) Occom preaching in Whitefield's Tabernacle, London; (3) First meeting of Trustees at Wyman Tavern, Keene, New Hampshire, October 12, 1770; (4) Wheelock and his family at Hanover, (a) ten little Indians, (b) prayers in the forest; (5) The first Commencement at Dartmouth, (a) tub scene, " 500 gallons of New England rum," (b) Governor Wentworth's visit; (6) Return of Captain John Wheelock and his company after Burgoyne's surrender; (7) Defence of the libraries against the university professors; (8) Daniel Webster pleading the college case at Washington.

On the morning of the twenty-sixth a great crowd in the church heard a brilliant historical address, " The Origins of Dartmouth College ", by Reverend Francis Brown, D. D., and saw Lord Dartmouth receive the honorary degree of LL. D. In the afternoon, which was stormy, a portion of the exercises was again held in the church, where Charles F. Mathewson, '82, gave a brief, but pungent address, and Lord Dartmouth made a perfectly expressed little speech of appreciation for the reception of himself and his family. The procession then moved to Eleazar Wheelock's grave, and over that plain old box of stone President Tucker spoke a few words in his always inspiring manner. A few moments later at the gaunt and ruined foundations of the old Dartmouth Hall, the earl with a silver trowel pressed the mortar in place on the corner-stone of the new. "And now, in the name of the Father, Son and Holy Ghost, I declare this corner-stone well and duly laid. *Floreat et haec nostra domus esto perpetua*", he said. A gallant peal from the chapel bells mercifully drowned out the mutterings of the assemblage's endeavors to turn the strange language into working English.

At the inevitable dinner, held in College Hall, there was an unusual amount of good talk. Honorable Elihu Root, President Eliot of Harvard, President Tyler of William and Mary, Honorable Charles T. Gallagher, Governor Bachelder, Doctor Charles A. Eastman and Lord Dartmouth were the speakers. President Tucker was at his best as master of the toasts. The earl, to those who had not known his English reputation, was a blithesome surprise as a wit on this occasion.

In all the marvelous material advance of President Tucker's administration, the problem of efficiency in scholarship was not neglected. For one thing, the loose system of electives that had let men browse around in totally disconnected fields was tightened very considerably. A so-called "group" system was adopted in 1902, both as to requirements for entrance to the college and as to subject matter to be studied, once within it. For the curriculum, the student was compelled to continue in freshman year the subjects he presented for admission; after that year, he was required to arrange his electives among three groups, so that one subject known as a " major " should be pursued for three years in one group, and so that one subject called a " minor " should be pursued for two years in each of the other two groups. This made prescribed subjects and those restricted by groups about forty per cent. of the whole course. It also brought every man's selected subjects into some kind of harmonious whole. It gave him a fairly free choice in the kind of education he wanted, but made him stick to his choice.

Along with these changes came the abandonment of Greek as a requirement for admission or for the degree of A. B. The literature of the Hellenes was decapitated calmly and with no resulting outcry. Since Lord's or even Bartlett's time, the college way, as the ways of all other colleges, had traveled far from the Acropolis. Greek remains, but it is rapidly approaching practical oblivion. There are those who mourn the decline of the noble tongue and letters at Dartmouth; but even a strong college cannot make the scholastic fashions of its day.

The " Great Awakening " was a superb realization

of the possibilities of Dartmouth and of the hopes of all her sons, but it brought its penalties to the man from whose brain and heart it had proceeded. In 1907 President Tucker found that his physical condition made rest imperative. He had labored without stint and almost single-handed upon academic, financial, and administrative problems. He had traveled the country over many times, the inspiring evangel of Dartmouth's message to the world. He had transformed Dartmouth from a small New Hampshire institution to a national college. He had seen the number of undergraduate students rise from 315 to 1,107, and the total college enrolment from 431 to 1,233. He had increased the resident faculty from twenty-seven to eighty-four, and the whole number of college officers from forty-two to one hundred and seven. He had enlarged the plant from fifteen buildings to thirty-five, exclusive of many houses in the village built or bought for faculty residences.

He had beautified and improved the college settlement to an astonishing degree. He had enlarged the invested funds by nearly two million dollars and the value of the plant by nearly a million and a half. And he had created among the alumni, always notably loyal, a new spirit of unification, of sacrifice, of intense devotion to and pride in the college that

Dartmouth men believe has no counterpart any-where.

But the price of this great service was loss of health, and in March, 1907, Doctor Tucker presented his resignation to the trustees, consenting, however, to remain, with lessened duties, until a successor could be found. No one available appearing within two years, the president was imperative that his resignation be accepted.

In June, 1909, the trustees chose Ernest Fox Nichols, a distinguished investigator in experimental physics, whose work was known to both hemispheres, as president. Doctor Nichols was then a professor in Columbia, but he knew Dartmouth well, having occupied the chair of physics in the college from 1898 to 1903.

Doctor Nichols was inducted into office October 10, 1909, in Webster Hall, and for the first time a Dartmouth inauguration became an event of national academic importance. Delegates from ninety-five universities, colleges, and other institutions of learning, saw the new president receive the ancient charter, once held so firmly in Eleazar Wheelock's grasp, and the Governor John Wentworth silver punch-bowl of fragrant memory, but departed glory. Never had the old town even dreamed of such a riot of color, such a human kaleidoscope, as wound and swayed across the campus with the procession of learned gentlemen wearing their doctors' caps, gowns, and hoods. To the small boys of Hanover, it was a revelation of the utmost glories to which finite beings might attain; to the men of Dartmouth, it was a testimony of the new rank to which the "Great Awakening" had brought their college, the world's "growing conception", as Woodrow Wilson put it in speaking of Doctor Tucker, "of what the character and power of a single man can do."

On this occasion, Presidents Schurman, of Cornell; Van Hise, of the University of Wisconsin; Finley, of the College of the City of New York; Hyde, of Bowdoin; Buckham, of the University of Vermont; Faunce, of Brown; Butler, of Columbia; Wilson, of Princeton; Hadley, of Yale; Lowell, of Harvard, and Eliot, emeritus; Angell, ex-President of Michigan; Doctor Tucker and Governor Quinby were made Doctors of Law. Rarely had any platform borne so distinguished a company of men. It is interesting to recall now the words of Doctor Nichols in presenting one of the degrees: "Woodrow Wilson, lawyer, historian, student of politics, man of great strength of purpose."

The years are slipping away since that day, also made notable by the laying of the corner-stone of the new gymnasium. The college, with President Nichols as its able and sympathetic head, is still gaining prestige and strength. More men are coming to it; new buildings are arising for it; its resources are increasing. It has a plant valued in 1913 at $2,472,532, and total assets of $5,450,281. Its annual cost of administration is only $36,605, which, reckoned as a percentage of the total business carried on, is smaller than that of any other prominent college in the country. That this means economy with no loss of efficiency, any intelligent survey of the condition of things at Hanover proves beyond question. The ancient strength is unabated; the modern note is but its finer and larger expression.

CHAPTER XIII

" THE OLD TRADITIONS "

Men of Dartmouth, set a watch
Lest the old traditions fail!

SO wrote the laureate of the college out of the inspiration of his great love for Dartmouth. We know and he knew that some of the old traditions ought to have failed; as they have. But his meaning no Dartmouth man misses.

All colleges have their peculiar traditions; even the younger are rapidly making them from customs that, because of the constantly shifting population of students, seem ancient in a few years. It is very noticeable that what a class begins to do often seems to have been done always; and, conversely, that it not seldom believes it has originated some custom that really is hoary with age. It is, therefore, difficult to place a college tradition, to give it accurate age or even any dignity.

But Dartmouth has a varied and interesting storehouse of traditions, which deserve the name because of their very disappearance into obscurity. Such is the tradition of the Old Pine. It was a pleasant tale that came down from the past — how the redskin graduates of the days when the " whole curriculum was five hundred gallons of New England rum " were accustomed, at Commencement, to smoke their peace pipes or dance around the lordly trunk of the tree that dominated the hill behind the college for so many years. The tradition was fit enough to be true, and perhaps it was. Doctor J. W. Barstow, '46, says of the Old Pine that " its worship did not begin until 1848 or '49." The first recorded exercise around the tree was at Class Day in 1854, when the graduates, sitting about the base, heard an oration and a poem. From that day until the fall of the splendid old monarch in 1895, graduating classes smoked the final pipe around the tree, dashing their clays against its trunk as a parting tribute. The custom is continued at its stump, which is carefully preserved.

Fagging is a tradition that has had the curious fate at Hanover of having long existed, of having died, and then of having a resurrection. This form of servitude was regularly recognized in the old code of college rules of 1799, freshmen being ordered to fetch and carry " for all the Senior classes who have themselves served a freshmanship." But the freshmen made their services obnoxious by the easy means of doing everything with an assumed density, such as, when ordered to go to a shop with a dollar for pipes and tobacco, returning with ninety-nine pipes and a cent's worth of tobacco. In 1796 a new set of college rules ordered that freshmen be excused from going on errands if they wished.

For years thereafter fagging was never heard of. It has recently returned in a genial sort of style, and freshmen to-day beat the rugs and set up the furniture of sophomores in good-natured acceptance of a system that they realize will work to their advantage a year later. Still, it is interesting to conjecture what would have happened in the roaring "eighties" had a "Soph" ordered a "Freshie" to beat his carpet. A fight would have been needed to enforce the ultimatum. Nor would there have been any peaceable submission, as there seems to be to-day, to the edict that freshmen must wear a distinctive cap as "his badge of servitude and his emblem of meekness."

Manifestly the relations between the two lower classes have lost the ferocity of more ancient times. And there is no doubt that one of the prime reasons for this is the disappearance of the cane-rush, which died as a genuine function in the middle "eighties."

This rush reached its most glorious estate in the fall of 1883, when it was prepared for in thoroughly scientific fashion. Every man of both classes was stripped to the waist, and the freshmen were deluged with olive oil at the hands of the juniors in the " gym." A minute after this ministration, the freshman band had formed a solid circle in the street, which was lined with the equipages of the country folk come in to see the fight, the men of the two upper classes, and most of the townspeople. In the center were three giants holding the hickory cane. The situation grew tense, when suddenly, with a terrifying yell, the cohorts of '86 dashed out from Reed Hall and, in wedge form, hit the round mass of '87 with a bone-crushing bang.

Up and down the street in the choking, rasping dust and the fierce September heat the oily contest raged for two mortal hours. Men fell out unconscious, only to be revived by buckets of cold water lavished upon them by the solicitous juniors. Trousers were torn to shreds, making necessary the retirement of the feminine spectators. Slowly the surging, writhing mass of greasy humanity somehow gravitated toward Reed Hall, until, with one final burst of power, the strong men of '86 shook off the freshmen and forced the cane through the doorway. The " Sophs " had won, as they always did in those days. Discipline and the solidarity of a year's acquaintance proved too much for untrained strength. In less than fifteen minutes, however, the freshmen, revived, bathed and clothed, were strutting across the campus, each sporting some sort of cane. The right to carry one had been strenuously earned.

Gone with the cane-rush is "Freshmen beer", and gone for the good of the college. This traditional entertainment was supposed to be the joyous compliment of the just-entered class to the others above it — a tribute to the powers that were for allowing freshmen to exist. The malt refreshment was usually brought up from "down river" in a couple of huge barrels and in some way hoisted into "Bed-bug Alley", the longitudinal hallway on the third floor of old Dartmouth. There, a barrel horsed up at either end, the bibulous portion of the college would make a night of it, swilling the dreadful brew until nature rebelled, faithfully believing that the occasion was an enjoyable one and that freshman honor had been gallantly maintained. Greater discretion finally caused the abandonment of the orgy; if beer is not wholly unknown at Hanover to-day, it is certainly more sensibly distributed.

The college cheer — the resounding "Wah-Hoo-Wah; Wah-Hoo-Wah; Da-di-di-Dartmouth, Wah-

Hoo-Wah, Tige-r-r-r — " — is to-day traditional; yet it is not ancient, unless one may believe that Eleazar's aborigines approximated to it in moments of fire-watered enthusiasm. Colder history records that it was the invention of Daniel A. Rollins, of the class of 1879. He was a genius for uniting the Indian flavor of a yell with sonorous power. No college has anything like it in fitness of sentiment as applied to origins. Unfortunately, of late years the cheer has been all but ruined and certainly made unintelligible by an over-increased speed in giving it. It has lost its swing, its power, and its meaning, and has become a mere jumble of barks. We may hope, however, that the spirit of artistic fitness of things, which is now coming upon the new Dartmouth, may yet summon back the Indian ghost of old " Wah-Hoo-Wah ", and return him to his place at the head of all college cheers.

Another supremely picturesque feature of Dartmouth student life of thirty years ago, whose passing is recalled with regret, was the ceremony of obsequies over mathematics. In its first form this was a burial, and its general nature may best be learned from a programme of 1872, issued by the sophomore class, whose function it was to inter the hated books at the end of their enforced acquaintance with them.

THE STORY OF DARTMOUTH

IN HISTORIAM

FUNERAL OBSEQUIES
OF
MATTHEW - MATICS.

This precious child was launched upon a frowning and unappreciative humanity September 1st A. D. 1870, and after a brief but brilliant career came to an untimely end May 6th, A. D. 1872.

"SIT TIBI TERRA LEVIS"

The procession will form in front of the Chapel at 10 P. M. and under the supervision of the Marshal will accompany the remains to their final resting-place in the following order:

I. Band.
II. Guard of Honor.
III. Pall Bearers supporting the *bier*.
IV. Near relatives.

ORDER OF EXERCISES
MUSIC.

Oration—Theme—$X = \infty$ Samuel L. Powers.

MUSIC.

Poem — The functions of
  Mathematics   Henry F. Chase.

"THE OLD TRADITIONS"

Funeral Ode   Henry H. Hart.

During the singing of the Ode, the rituals will be performed. At the close of which a salute will be fired into the grave, and amid salvos of musketry and the wailing of the bereaved friends, each member of the class will pay his last tribute of affection and esteem to the memory of the departed.

At the close of these exercises, the class in individual procession, as components of a great mathematical force, will seek solace in the limits of space. Quod Erat Demonstrandum.

When this travesty on burial was finally forbidden by the faculty, the change was made — with the ease and ingenuity of college boys — to cremation, a very much finer spectacle. The last ceremony of burning was held in the spring of 1884. It was weirdly attractive. Preceded by a band groaning out a solemn dirge, eight students dressed as Roman priests carried the books on a bier. The class followed, bearing torches, each man wearing a long black robe over the head with holes cut for eyes, nose, and mouth. A number of imps, clad in red, disported themselves about the cortege as it marched around the campus and thence to a huge funeral pyre inside the fence. As fire was touched to the wood, the books were hurled into the flames with yells of exultation, and a wild hand-in-hand dance celebrated their final consumption. This wonderfully picturesque custom has its modern counterpart in the cremation of freshman caps at the close of a first class year in college; but it lacks the decorative features of the older function.

One of the most pleasing of the ancient Hanoverian customs, because it reveals sentiment of a rare and compelling kind, is that of " Singing out the Seniors " the week before Commencement. For this parting God-speed to the men about to go into the world, the whole college gathers in chapel for the last exercise for the year in that place. The simplicity of it all is most impressive. There is a scripture reading, a prayer, an anthem by the choir and then the singing by the seniors of the time-honored hymn, beginning:

> Come let us anew our journey pursue;
> Roll 'round with the year,
> And never stand still till the Master appear.

The age of this solemn observance is unknown. A member of the class of 1846 says that it was in vogue in 1843, as long established and recognized.

Of less antiquity, but now a genuine tradition, is

the senior " Wet-Down ", which takes the form of
a great barrel of lemonade set up on the campus
after the " Sing-Out." Of this harmless concoction,
which custom rigidly requires to be without a
" stick ", the seniors and juniors are given to drink,
while the sophomores and freshmen struggle to
tip the barrel over in derision of its mildness. All
this may seem rather childish and unsophisticated
to the " clubman " of the city college, but at Dartmouth the " old traditions " give vitality and
virility to many a naive custom, because it is still
remembered that " there were mighty men of old "
who were not ashamed to love and perpetuate
them.

Commencements as a whole, however, have
vastly improved in decorum and taste in fifty
years, mainly because the " circusing " of the annual
event for the outside world has long ceased. " It
is now almost Commencement ", wrote a student
to his brother in 1824. " Three days more will
bring us to that day, when the devil reigns pre-
dominant." Lord observes that " in the height
of its glory, and within the memory of the older
alumni, this occasion combined with the genuine
and refined pleasures of a great literary gathering
all the external attractions appropriate to a fair or
a general muster of the olden time. The din of

preparation for these began with the break of day on Monday by the construction of booths in choice spots about the southwestern corner of the Green. During that day and the next every public conveyance brought its contribution till all the houses of the village, both public and private, were filled with guests.

"On the morning of Wednesday all approaches to the village were crowded with vehicles of every description, and numerous foot passengers as well, all hurrying in to see the fun. By this time every available spot along the southern extremity of the square would be occupied with a booth of a trader, and, as the day passed, travelling adventurers swarmed in with their carts and bivouacked on the spot. The night that followed was enlivened with their lamps and the buzz of preparation, and sometimes with the persuasions of the students, who, not relishing their presence, attempted to induce them to depart. The surrounding country was emptied into Hanover. Instances are not wanting of persons who have attended fifty consecutive Commencements.

"The peddlers, the auctioneers, the jugglers and the shows with their attendant throngs would spread far up toward the meeting house, and with the cider, the strong beer openly sold, and the stronger drink scarcely concealed, toward evening the crowds would wax ruder and the turmoil more furious, until it not seldom resulted in a brawl, so that all orderly people breathed freer if the usual thunder-shower dispersed the noisy and profane rabble."

As late as 1845, Commencement was more or less attended by a raree-show. One of the Hanover residents relates in his diary for that year: " July 31st. The annual Commencement this day and a fine fair day too. The smallest literary procession that I have noticed for several years — but an uncommon rush of all kinds of people from the circumstance that there was uncommon attractions for them. A somewhat extensive Menagerie of wild animals (in most miserable plight however). The Boston Brass band of musicians, and the famous foreign Violin player named Ole Bull, and 4 Albinoes or white negroes. Every thing to pick away money and lead the mind of people from the great concerns of eternity and their duties of charity to their needy fellow citizens and the perishing heathen. Even clergymen were so enraptured that they could not resist the invitation to hand out their half dollar to hear him scrape his catgut — and another quarter to hear the brass band perform."

The senior spreads of that day were bountiful, if

not esthetic. A visitor to the same Commencement wrote: "At nine o'clock in the evening we went up to the assembly rooms in the new College (Reed Hall) where the graduating class held their select Levee. It was very tastefully decorated and the table most magnificently spread. We had peaches, apricots, grapes, oranges, raisins, figs, nuts of all kinds, pickled fish, water melons a foot and a half or two feet long, cakes, ice-cream, tea, coffee and lemonade. The students gave this instead of a ball. Kendall's band played, and all went off well."

Traditional "characters" have always abounded at Dartmouth, as with every college set in a small village where the all in all is the institution itself. Most of these worthies have left no history, no memories, even. Others, still haunting the thoughts of Dartmouth men yet living, will again visualize themselves at the touch of suggestion. There was "Hod" Frary, for instance, the keeper of the old Dartmouth Hotel, one of whose cherished habits it was to carve the roasts on a table in the corner of the dining-room and every now and then, in full sight of the guests, wipe his enormous knife across a vest encrusted with the grease and blood of ages. The students had a theory that "Hod" did this to discourage appetite on the part of his boarders, and thus make his table d'hôte the more profitable.

"THE OLD TRADITIONS"

There was the quaint old "Professor of Dust and Ashes", whose loved and pompous duty it was to clear the ancient recitation rooms of the litter strewn about by the students, and to build the fires in the big box stoves that heated these abodes of the muses. His name was Haskell, and he lived across the way from the old Rood House, where was located, in his day, the "elegant" young ladies' boarding school kept by the Argus-eyed Misses Sherman, and known as the "Sherman Nunnery." The good "Professor" has long been dust and ashes himself, but his memory is still cherished among the older alumni.

There was "Old Dud", who, with his flotilla of ancient stage-coaches swung on leather springs and drawn up in gallant array at the station, "Nawich 'nd 'Anover" was the official welcomer of returning Dartmouth men for a period of nearly forty years. "Old Dud", the magnate of all stage drivers, the man who would in these days run grave risk of being prosecuted by the Commerce Commission for restraint of interstate transportation. "Old Dud", the friend of everybody and everybody's friend!

There was "Lil" Carter, the Delmonico of the middle "eighties", in Hanover. The maker of the best oyster stews and ice-cream that ever tickled the palates and depleted the pocketbooks of college students in any town, big or little. A cheerful truster, withal. There was no occasion to growl at the high cost of living while " Lil " was in business. At first he kept open house in the Tontine Block, where several of the secret society halls were then located, but when that was burned, he established his restaurant in the second story of his stable. His customers had to admit that the flavor of his food suffered somewhat from the change. There was a sort of ammonia tang to what one drank and a distinctly horsey aroma about what one ate. But " Lil ", like a gentleman, made up for this by giving bigger portions of everything and extending longer credit all around.

There was " Kib ", proprietor of " Kibling's Op'ry House," on College Street,

> That thespian den
> Where tragic ham-fats roared on 6 by 10,
> Where dear Hank White retold his minstrel jest,
> And Barnaby's " cork leg " led all the rest.
> Where the " Mikado " burst upon the town,
> And college fiddlers squeaked the chorus down.

" Kib's " temple of art was all too often the scene of histrionic efforts that should never have been made. But if a guilty company tarried a second night, its doom was swift and certain. The sophomores would gather to a man outside the hall, promptly at eight, equipped with tin horns, cowbells and band instruments, and blare away until the wretched actors inside would give up the struggle to be heard and dismiss their audience. This was not strictly gentlemanly, judged by the rules of more polite society, but it was a protest at being duped, the only effective one the boys knew, since there were no other censors of the drama in Hanover then.

" Kib " also maintained in one corner of his establishment a wretched little bar-room, where with hardened soul he dispensed his terrible " ink " and " resin " as, with malignant glee, he termed whisky and beer. Later he faced a lifetime in jail on accumulated sentences for " selling ", but a too-lenient law set him free after a brief period of servitude. " Kib " was the last easily accessible and defiant rumseller in Hanover.

And then there was the illustrious Daniel Pratt, the " Great American Traveler ", property of other colleges, also, because of his love for them all and his peripatetic habits among them. The dear old man was once made the hero of a great procession at Hanover, being escorted from the Dartmouth Hotel to the old chapel. There, with colossal gravity, the students conferred upon him the honorary degree of C. O. D. Pratt then delivered himself of a wonderful oration on the " Vocabulaboratory of the World's History." It is related that after the address was over, as he came out on the chapel steps, some disturbance was caused, and, brave man and chevalier though he was, he became frightened and started across the campus like a deer with the whole college in full cry after him.

Eheu, fugaces! Times change, and men and things change with them. The familiars of yesterday are the traditions of to-day, and the traditions of to-morrow are to-day in the making. Dartmouth, by reason of her very distinctive flavor, will not soon cease to be a college of " the old traditions." Some will be born, will flourish, and will die. Some will live always. Dartmouth's sons have set a watch.

CHAPTER XIV

" DARTMOUTH OUT - O' - DOORS "

DARTMOUTH is to-day preeminently the college of the " out-o'-doors." This distinction has not come to it entirely by reason of its superb location, where mountains, hills, and glades; forests and streams; a lordly river at its feet and lovely lakes within easy reach give it a setting incomparable for the casual stroll or the strenuous, long-distance " hike." For more than a century these prodigally beautiful gifts of nature encircled Dartmouth, yet there has not until recently been any genuine or general use of them.

A generation ago the few men who " tramped " in spring or autumn were rare and queer specimens to the majority. The rigors of winter were for the most part evaded by close adherence to stoves. A cross-country trip over the snow would have been regarded as an expedition of lunatics. Toboggans, skis and snow-shoes were unknown; sleighing was not popular; coasting languished, and skating was generally impossible by reason of the heavy snow-falls. The prevailing attitude toward winter was accurately expressed in Richard Hovey's:

For the wolf wind is whining in the doorways,
And the snow drifts deep along the road,
And the ice-gnomes are marching from their Norways,
And the great white cold walks abroad.
(Boo-oo-o! pass the bowl.)
    For here by the fire
    We defy frost and storm.
    Ha, ha! we are warm
    And we have our hearts' desire.

To-day, thanks to the activities of the Dartmouth Outing Club and to a new appreciation of the joys of the open country, all seasons bring large numbers of students into the " out-o'-doors " and the formidable old Hanover winter itself is now enlivened by one of the finest and most popular celebrations of the college year, the Winter Carnival.

The first exponent of " Dartmouth out-o'-doors " was John Ledyard, that original genius and adventurous soul of the class of 1776, who roamed the world in marvellous fashion for his day, and finally died in Africa, as he was preparing to cross that continent. Ledyard arrived in Hanover in a sulky, which he had driven through the wilderness roads from Hartford. That he and his equipage made a sensation when they reached the college may be taken for granted. " Both the horse and the sulky ", says Sparks, " gave evident tokens of having known better days, and the dress of their owner was pe-

Wilson Hall (Library)

culiar, bidding equal defiance to symmetry of proportion and to the fashion of the times. In addition to the traveller himself, this ancient vehicle was burdened with a quantity of calico for curtains, and other articles to assist in theatrical exhibitions, of which he was very fond. . . . The stage was fitted up, and plays were acted, in which Ledyard personated the chief characters. ' Cato ' was among the tragedies brought out upon the boards, and Ledyard acted the part of old Syphax, wearing a long gray beard and a dress suited to his notion of the costume of a Numidian prince."

Whether Ledyard loved nature with an unusual passion, or merely desired a lark in the open now and then, we do not know. But it is recorded that in the midwinter of 1772–1773, he, with Wheelock's consent, persuaded several of the students to camp out with him in the snow in the wilds of the " Velvet Rocks ", two miles east of the college. The snow was three feet deep, and drifted. The party went in couples on snow-shoes, and reaching the summit with some labor, built a fire, ate their supper, and each couple prepared for the night by scraping away the snow and laying a bed of evergreen boughs and a blanket. One then lying down, his partner drew over him a second blanket, buried him in snow, and then crawled in by his side. They passed, they said, quite a comfortable night, and were at home in time for prayers by candle-light in the morning.

Chafing at last under old Eleazar's rigid discipline, and objecting particularly to the compulsion of blowing the conch horn in his turn to summon the students to various exercises, Ledyard determined to abscond. In May, 1773, while the president was in the " down-country ", he cut a huge pine near the banks of the river, and from it fashioned a dug-out canoe fifty feet long and three feet wide. This stalwart craft, rigged with a woven willow shelter in the stern, was launched with the help of classmates, and in it Ledyard, with dried venison for food and a bearskin for covering at night, paddled down the Connecticut to Hartford, one hundred and forty miles away, narrowly escaping with his life at the thundering maelstrom of Bellows Falls. A great stone, with bronze tablet, now marks the spot where this first of Dartmouth's " gentleman adventurers " cut the tree for his craft.

But although now and again men have loved the silent places about the college town, where one can be remote and almost in the wilderness in an hour's walk, the great green and white " out-o'-doors " waited a hundred and forty-one years for the forming of an association that should at last bring a large number of pioneers into the open with the bonds of enthusiasm and energy.

It was in January, 1910, that F. H. Harris, of the class of 1911, " the lone ski-runner ", was inspired, on one of his expeditions over the snow, with the idea that the old time Hanoverian conception of winter was all wrong; that it was not a dread time for the close embrace of the steam radiator, but a glorious opportunity for the making of redder blood, more powerful appetites, and sounder sleep. He issued a call to the wild in the *Dartmouth*. Fifty men replied. The Dartmouth Outing Club had its birth forthwith. Skis, snow-shoes and toboggans suddenly became profitable articles of merchandise. From fifty, the membership of the club quickly grew to hundreds.

Out of the new organization's fertile activities came the Winter Carnival, which now attracts crowds of visitors, including the inevitable, enthusiastic girls, to enjoy the ski and snow-shoe dashes and cross-country runs, the hockey games, and the ski-jumps. " The great white cold walks abroad ", as in Hovey's time, and often to the pace of twenty degrees below zero, at these carnivals; but nobody is daunted, nobody is frozen, and the feminine contingent transfers itself from furs, mackinaws, sweaters, and toques to the silks and satins of evening dress for the Carnival Ball in the commons with as good grace as if the dance were in Boston or New York.

The chief glory of the Outing Club, however, and a thing that is bound to make a race of Dartmouth men still stauncher of body, cleaner of morals, and more thoughtful of mind, is the trail and cabin system that has come into being naturally and consistently with the splendid theater nature has given the college men for their " out-o'-door " performances.

The beginning of this unique course of education in the semi-wilderness was the excellent cabin on the side of Moose Mountain, a fine and dominating eminence eight miles northeast of the campus. Through the enthusiastic interest and labors of Mr. Franklin P. Shumway, of Boston, the alumni gave the six hundred dollars necessary to erect the shelter, which was dedicated by President Nichols on May 30, 1913. Here, close to a cold and picturesque mountain torrent, as many as thirty students may gather about the roaring logs in the big stone fireplace; may sleep in bunks lined with fir-balsam; may prepare the good, honest " grub " of the camper in the well-appointed kitchen, and may look out over the beautiful world for a brief interval between classrooms, into the setting sun or the young moon, and be the better for doing it.

Next in this chain is Cube Mountain, a still nobler
hill ten miles to the north of Moose. Here another
Dartmouth cabin has been erected, thanks again to
Mr. Shumway's persuasive ways with the alumni.
Further still will be a cabin in the Agassiz Basin,
near Moosilauke, land for which has been given by
Reverend J. E. Johnson, of the class of 1866, who
had presented the club, in 1913, with his hundred-
acre place, " Sky-Line Farm " in Littleton, including
a good house. This point completes the northern
trail for Dartmouth, since from Littleton or from
Agassiz Basin the " hiker " into the heart of the
White Mountains may find plenty of Appalachian
Club and other cabins ready for service.

The next developments are expected to be toward
the east, perhaps on Mount Cardigan, and to the
west into the foothills of the Green Mountains.
There is no limit to the magnificent range of outing
possibilities in every point of the compass. Health
and strength and manly love for the open beckon at
every turn of the year, and from the " groves of the
academy " Dartmouth men in constantly greater
numbers are going out into the groves of the Om-
nipotent for something no finite theorems or mental
gymnastics of the class or lecture-room can possibly
give them.

The " out-o'-door " activities that take the form

of organized athletics are, of course, older than the present remarkable spirit of the trail; yet modern enough, as compared with the life of the college. The ancient worthies did not look with much favor on useless and non-productive games. The first code of college laws set forth its desires thus:

In order that the channel of their diversions may be turned from that which is puerile, such as playing with balls, bowls, and other ways of diversion, as have been necessarily gone into by students in other places, for want of an opportunity to exercise themselves in that which is more useful, . . . it is earnestly recommended to the students . . . that they turn the course of their diversions, and exercises for their health, to the practice of some manual arts, or cultivation of gardens and other lands at the proper hours of leisure.

Eleazar Wheelock was a thrifty soul who realized the advantage of employing student energies to the turning out of vegetables for the benefit of the college.

But games persisted, in more or less fugitive fashion. The Indians had sports of their own and pursued them as long as they remained at Dartmouth. Wickets were in fashion in 1790, if we may trust a naive engraving of the college grounds at that period. Football of the "Old Division", free-for-all, "kick-as-kick-can" style flourished for many years, and was played up to 1850 with an inflated bladder inside a leather case. For the gymnastic enthusiasts a frame was set up in 1852 back of the observatory. This contrivance, boasting only two ropes with rings and a horizontal bar, was known as the " Freshman Gallows ", by reason of a tradition, which has an apocryphal flavor, that a member of one lowly class brought himself to an untimely end by too strenuous work upon it.

Of the athletic sports now existent at Hanover, baseball is the oldest. The first college nine was organized in 1866, " to supply a deficiency ", said the *Aegis* of that time, " occasioned by the lack of interest displayed in the football game. . . . It is our belief that football must cease to exist as a college game. The time and advancing interests of old Dartmouth demand it."

That nine beat Concord and Portsmouth, but was defeated by Amherst, 40 to 10, on its own ground. The first game with Harvard was played in 1869, and Harvard's seasoned veterans won, 38 to 0. That old score has been paid off by Dartmouth victories many times since then, but never in such impressive numerical fashion, for the days of enormous scores and appalling error figures soon passed. Dartmouth's baseball record has always been honorable and still is, though the old-time interest in

the game, which was overwhelmingly keen in the
" eighties ", is now at a much lower ebb among the
non-playing students.

Curiously enough, intercollegiate rowing, now and
for a long time extinct at Hanover, in spite of the
great river near by, ran baseball a close second in
point of age. It began with a spontaneous " craze ",
so the athletic records say, in the autumn of 1872.
Eaton, '75, and Paul, Lawrence, and Underhill, '73,
were the pioneers in the movement. In the winter
enough money was raised to build a boathouse, hire
a trainer, and buy a six-oared cedar shell from the
famous Elliott, of Greenpoint, Long Island. An
old professional " champ " named John Biglin was
the trainer. He selected a crew of " raw beef and
bloody bone giants ", who in spite of their crudity
as oarsmen, brought the Dartmouth shell in fourth
among nine at the Springfield regatta of '73. Next
year the crew finished fourth at Saratoga, being
beaten by Columbia, Wesleyan, and Harvard. In
1875 the Hanoverians were again fourth, five sec-
onds behind Harvard and beating Yale, with " Bob "
Cook at stroke oar.

From that moment of what was rightfully considered a good deal of a triumph, Dartmouth has
never put a 'varsity shell into the water. A tremendous snowfall in the winter of 1877 crushed in

the boathouse and smashed the shell; seemingly it crushed the heart out of rowing, in which the collegians had played so creditable a rôle. This form of athletics appears to be dead at Hanover, and no one can be found there who will venture to predict its resurrection.

Modern football — " Rugby ", as it was called in its early days of evolution among the American colleges — was late in arriving at Hanover. Harvard, Princeton, and Yale had for some time been at their triangular annual contests before Dartmouth knew the pigskin well. When at various times the matter was broached, the faculty, who tolerated the fierce cane-rush, demurred on the ground that the game was too " rough." Even a part of the students frowned on it, though not for that reason, certainly. They feared that the pastime was too much an aping of effete England and that it would tend to produce a race of effeminates! They were soon to see that notion exploded with loud reverberations over the Hanover plain.

In spite of opposition, the football feeling gained steadily. Clarence Howland, '84, did much to establish the new game. A magnificent player and a man of means, he helped the cause physically and financially. Exeter men began to come up to the college with football training. In 1880 the elements for the sport were strong enough to force the organization of the Dartmouth Rugby Football Association, and an eleven was put on the field. There were no intercollegiate games that year, but in 1881 two contests were arranged with Amherst, Dartmouth winning the first and tying the second. On November 9, 1882, came the first game with Harvard, and the score of 53 to 0 showed the wearers of the green that they knew very little of the game. But that catastrophe, too, was amply avenged in 1903, when the Dartmouth eleven, perhaps the most powerful that ever swept over a gridiron, dedicated the Stadium with a Harvard defeat, 11 to 0.

After the first Harvard game, however, things looked bad for football at Hanover. The *Dartmouth*, under the heading " Rugby Is Dead ", said editorially: " It is our sad duty to conduct the melancholy obsequies. . . . There was no doubt, no mystery about its death, and an inquest is totally unnecessary . . . and now if there is any other game that Dartmouth can play better than football, it would be well to encourage it."

But football did not die. It survived even the ponderous trouncing administered by Yale on Dartmouth's ground in 1884, when the score was 113 to 0 for the blue. It survived many another defeat, victories coming along in due time. Under the coaching of such men as McCornack, Folsom, O'Connor, and Cavanaugh, the elevens of Dartmouth have been made formidable fighting aggregations and have long since been reckoned with as among the best in the college world every season. From the humble beginnings at Harvard, when a few of the faithful sat along the side-lines to cheer the eleven in its regular defeats, Dartmouth finally arrived at the importance of being able to draw a crowd of forty thousand spectators to the Stadium to witness the annual battle between the crimson and the green.

In field and track athletics, Dartmouth has not until recently cut a very important figure among the largest colleges. In her old-time class, however, she has long been customarily victorious, winning the New England Intercollegiate championship (Harvard and Yale have never been members) for the great majority of years in which the association has existed.

The first local field meet was held in the fall of 1875, with such ancient exotics as the three-legged race, the sack race, and the wheelbarrow race on the list of events. The initial outside appearance of her athletes was at Glen Mitchell, New York, in July, 1876, when they won several events in a field consisting of Princeton, Yale, Cornell, Columbia,

Williams, Wesleyan, and the University of the City of New York. At Mott Haven, in 1877, a Dartmouth man won the half-mile and the quarter-mile. Dartmouth won the first meet of the New England Intercollegiate Athletic Association held at Charter Oak Park, Hartford, May 27, 1887.

Of late years Dartmouth has been consistently growing stronger in the " big " Intercollegiates, a result due partly to the splendid new " gym ", with its facilities for practising practically all of the outdoor sports in the depth of winter, and partly to the fine and inspiring labors of Harry Hillman, the track and field coach. The alumni control of athletics, established in 1892, has also been of great value as an inspiration toward success in all branches, as a financial ally, and as a wise guardian of what is clean and honorable in amateur sport. Dartmouth is to-day in the very first rank in her punctilious regard for pure athletics. It is not a pose, but a conviction. It governs the conduct of the sports just mentioned, as well as of tennis, golf, hockey, and basketball, in all of which good records have been made.

One more asset of " Dartmouth out-o'-doors ", unique and full of the most romantic possibilities, is the " Dartmouth Grant ", the splendid domain of twenty-six thousand acres of wild forest, moun-

The Alumni Gymnasium

tain, and stream up in the " North Country." This great territory lies in the northeast corner of New Hampshire, edging the State of Maine for eight miles. No shrieks of locomotives disturb its quiet, for the nearest railway station is thirty-two miles away. In its wilderness are five mountains more than two thousand feet high; two gloriously picturesque rivers, Swift Diamond and Dead Diamond; innumerable brooks, and all about the deep forest, broken only by the hundred-acre clearings for the " college farm " in the center of the tract and the " Davis farm " at the southeastern entrance to the property. On one of its rivers a canoe can float for twenty miles. Everywhere wild life abounds, but in peace, unharassed by gunpowder. Dartmouth protects her tenants under old Dame Nature's lease.

The future uses of this forest principality delight the imagination. What will the " Grant " see and be in a hundred years? In five hundred? Wilderness still, kept in virgin glory from the ravages of an advancing civilization, or the sylvan seat of a great department of the college? At present its utility is the furnishing of lumber under a wise system of modern forestry. It will never be " stripped ", let us believe, to naked land and savage rock.

What an opportunity is here for the school of forestry that Dartmouth may one day establish. What a realm of delight for the summer camp of some Dartmouth Outing Club of the future, that may " hike " in a body to the enchanted land of the northern " out-o'-doors." Happy the college, and happy the college men, who can still carry the ancient seal into their own lands and there let its legend speak again, and as appropriately as in the days of the founding: " *Vox Clamantis in Deserto*."

CHAPTER XV

DARTMOUTH is still a college. It adopts men into the academic family on fairly easy terms, but it compels them to prove their intellectual and moral fitness to remain, or out they go without much ceremony. Every year a sizable band of lazy or over-confident freshmen is given its passports. Sometimes this coterie contains the most promising athletic material of a class, but that consideration weighs not at all in the councils of the faculty. The Governor John Wentworth charter is older than the Alumni Gymnasium, and the charter has certain things to say about the general intent of the college. Those things are still respected. Men are still personally trained in classroom recitations as well as in lectures and examinations. They are still held to the performance of a definite excellence in mental work as represented by professorial figures. If they object to this as a form of ancient inquisition, they are at liberty to resign, and often they are asked to.

As to what men do at Dartmouth, then, it may be

said that primarily they work at such varied forms of the higher education as they may select out of a liberal variety. But they work, or they know Hanover but briefly.

Of student interests outside the regular curriculum there is today a wide choice, suited for men of all sorts of tastes, compared with the narrow range of things to do a generation, or less, ago. There is no doubt that the students of the present conduct themselves more sensibly than in older times because there are so many congenial outlets for their particular kinds of effervescence. Turkey-stealing, rum-drinking and horning have gone into the dustbin of disused traditions in favor of Outing Club trips, or dramatic performances or Social Service or of half a dozen other activities of as much appeal, but less potentiality for trouble. And if any " old timer ", any product of the Iron Age at Hanover, should chance to fear that the change in student avocations and pleasures is in danger of producing a race of prigs and weaklings, a visit to the old town in Winter Carnival week would be sufficient to drive that dismal notion entirely from his head. The ancient and highly characteristic idea of Dartmouth manhood seems as potent and as living as ever it was.

Men have more luxuries, of course, than their

fathers even dreamed of. They are no longer living like a lot of anchorites, for the college has seen to it that they are comfortably housed. The great increase in handsome and well-equipped fraternity houses in recent years has also changed the manner of living to some extent, but not to the cliquey and dangerous length seen at some other colleges, for here again the wisdom of President Tucker was wonderfully manifested when he persuaded the trustees to rule that no fraternity house should contain more than fourteen men and that none should set a regular table. It has thus been made impossible that any set of students exist within a fraternity shell. Somewhere, three times a day, they must all associate with other men.

If the problems of fraternity scholarship, which is proven poorer than that of non-fraternity men at Dartmouth, and the perennial nuisance of the " chinning " season could be settled as adequately and simply, the powers that be at Hanover would be happier. However, the fraternity question is in process of better regulation than ever before, partly through frank and free conferences of society delegates with President Nichols, and partly from a feeling among the " frat " men that there may be something in their honorable traditions of scholarship and literature, after all.

There are now eighteen Greek letter societies in
the college proper, the oldest of which is Psi Upsilon,
founded at Dartmouth in 1842, and the youngest
Delta Sigma Rho, established in 1910. One, the
Kappa Kappa Kappa, is local only.[1] These chapters,
which include about sixty per cent. of the students,
have always maintained their connection with the
parent fraternities. None has deteriorated into an
expelled, independent club bearing a parody of the
old mother's name and active chiefly as a social
organization playing fool pranks in public. In that
respect the history and the present status of the
fraternities at Dartmouth is honorable. Men may
not take them very seriously as uplifts, but they do
not degrade them into mere accessories for eating
and drinking and the doing of idiotic " stunts."

Four senior societies make the sum total of Dartmouth's desires in this respect. The Sphinx, founded
in 1886, has an effective Eygptian mausoleum as a
meeting-place; the Casque and Gauntlet, one year
younger, owns and occupies a prim, but pleasant

[1] The Greek letter societies in the order of their founding at Dart-
mouth are: Psi Upsilon, 1842; Kappa Kappa Kappa, 1842; Alpha
Delta Phi, 1846; Delta Kappa Epsilon, 1853; Theta Delta Chi, 1869;
Phi Delta Theta, 1884; Beta Theta Pi, 1889; Sigma Chi, 1893; Phi
Kappa Psi, 1896; Phi Gamma Delta, 1901; Chi Phi, 1902; Phi Sigma
Kappa, 1905; Kappa Sigma, 1905; Sigma Phi Epsilon, 1909; Sigma Nu,
1907; Sigma Alpha Epsilon, 1908; and Delta Sigma Rho, 1910.

old-fashioned dwelling-house, lately much improved, on the busy and valuable corner opposite College Hall. The Dragon, still younger, occupies the ancient, square "Tri-Kappa" Hall. The Round Robin is purely literary. Election to these organizations is a distinction highly prized by each junior class, though there is nothing of sycophantish log-rolling for " making " the senior societies that has been condemned in some other colleges.

Palaeopitus is another Dartmouth institution that has won a very important place in the college life. This is the student governing body of the college. A board of eleven members of the senior class, it is the Hague Conference of the under-graduate body and the official intermediary between the faculty administration and the students. Tra-dition alone is responsible for raising the Palaeo-pitus to its present high position, and upon the pres-tige that it has attained it is wholly dependent for its power. Election to this body is probably the most substantial recognition of ability and in-tegrity that a class can confer on one of its mem-bers. It may be safely said that petty politics and fraternity rivalries rarely interfere with the election of the best possible men from the successive classes to this surprisingly influential group of men. The relation of the Palaeopitus to the college is unique among student councils. It has never received any specific powers from the administration or the student body. It has no definite duties to perform except those developed by the usage of years. In spite of this fact, the resolutions and suggestions of the Palaeopitus have all the force of laws. It is now an institution that neither undergraduates nor faculty would like to see abandoned.

Phi Beta Kappa survives as a reward for the first scholars in each senior class — for all receiving a rank of eighty-five, to be exact. The ancient dame with the watch-key came to Hanover in 1787, from Cambridge. In those days she was a secretive soul, with solemn oaths of initiation, a mystic cipher and strange symbols. These attributes have long since disappeared, as well as the term-time meetings of the society. In its old-time state it was distinguished every third year by a Phi Beta Kappa oration on the day before Commencement, and some of the greatest of American minds have had their say on these occasions.

For men who feel the "furor scribendi" at Hanover there are means of expression adequate enough, if not over plentiful. The *Dartmouth*, the triweekly college newspaper, annually calls forth a good-sized crowd of freshman "leg-men," eager to win a place on its staff. This venerable sheet, as such publications go, has had a continuous existence since 1867, when it was revived as a monthly after a suspension of twenty-six years. In 1875 it was made a weekly newspaper, and its character has more and more tended to that of a chronicler of and commentator on the college happenings to the exclusion of everything else. The *Dartmouth* is lively and enterprising, and occasionally prods the college moguls a bit sharply; but the freedom of the press is pretty well respected at Hanover, and nothing happens in the way of editorial repression.

The *Bema* is the direct descendant of the *Dartmouth Literary Monthly*, established in 1887, and later renamed the *Dartmouth Magazine*. It is young and pretty, with excellent illustrations, interesting departments and better than average stories and poems. " *Jack O' Lantern* ", the humorous monthly, gives the wits and the cartoonists their chief opportunity nowadays at Hanover, since the *Aegis*, the junior annual founded as a once-a-term magazine in 1858, but having its present form since 1871, has lost much of its former penchant for biting and sometimes brutal " grinds " on students and faculty. The *Dartmouth Alumni Magazine*, now six years old, is a valuable publication, covering the larger forms of college news very completely and reflecting editorially — and often briskly — the faculty attitude toward college events and student behavior.

The men who lean toward "Music, heavenly maid," are variously provided for. "The Handel Society of Dartmouth College", organized in 1807 "to improve and cultivate the taste, and promote true and genuine music and discountenance trifling, unfinished pieces", and which for many years was accounted one of the best choruses in New England, is dead. The College Choir in some measure fills its place. Those who yearn for the "trifling, unfinished pieces" may find solace in the Glee Club, with its guitar and mandolin attachments. Then the freshman who can play any instrument reasonably well is sure of a warm welcome to the college band and the orchestra. The annual musical comedies give many aspirants for vocal training and honors a field of some value.

The most remarkable development of student activities of recent years at Dartmouth is the rise and success of the Dramatic Association. This organization has broken entirely with the older tradition that college players must devote themselves to the generally trivial stuff produced by college writers. It presents, and produces with adequate scenery and costumes, such plays as Maeterlinck's "The Intruder", Lady Gregory's

" The Workhouse Ward "; Maurice Baring's " Katherine Parr "; Witter Bynner's " The Little King "; Carl Freybe's " On Leave of Absence "; W. F. Locke's " The Climax " and Macdonald Hasting's " The New Sin." In the spring of 1914 the association moved upon New York and gave " The Misleading Lady " for two matinees at the Fulton Theatre, where the piece was running professionally. The critics were unanimous in declaring this to be the best college student performance ever seen in New York. The usual feeling that college boys were masquerading in the spirit of a lark seemed to have been lost altogether in admiration of the sincerity and real dramatic values of the presentation.

That this new and extraordinary feeling for the art of the stage — well supported by the student body — is bound to have its effect in arousing a love for the best of drama and an incentive to serious play-writing at Dartmouth is not questioned anywhere. Despite the time and energy such work demands on the part of the men in college, the faculty wisely approves the movement, as giving a certain cultural bit of education that could be obtained in no other way.

For those who feel the call to public pronouncements minus stage accessories the Dartmouth

Forensic Union, with its annual triangular debating league with Williams and Brown, is accessible to men with highly developed platform ability. The Lincoln-Douglas Debating Society offers a wider field for the oratorically inclined, while " Le Cercle Français ", " El Centro Espanol " and the " Deutscher Verein " fill their customary places acceptably.

On the more serious, but by no means sanctimonious side of life at Hanover stands the Dartmouth Christian Association. This organization has thirty years of earnest and loyal work to its credit, and from its home in Bartlett Hall has gone forth an inspiration to manly living and commonsense Christianity. Many a great athlete, wearing the precious " D " on his breast, might also, appropriately enough, have added " C. A." to his badge of accomplishment.

The Christian Association men have of recent years extended the movement far outside the old-time bounds of Hanover. Good speakers, magnetic fellows, have taken up social service in many of the towns and villages and preparatory schools within a radius of forty miles. This is called " deputation " work. It is not too solemn. College songs, instrumental concerts and vaudeville " stunts " are often given at the meetings of young men in places outside Hanover. Then follows some simple, sincere

Reed and Bartlett Halls

talk on the advantages of high ideals, of fairness, clearness and unselfishness, the religious appeal coming last as the most impressioning feature of the gatherings. Boy Scout work and a night school for Poles at the mills of Wilder, just down the river, are other features of " deputation " activity. The *Aegis* says that up to March 31, 1913, more than three hundred different undergraduates had participated in one or more phases of the Association's work. Thus is regard for the welfare of " the other fellow " being inculcated in Dartmouth men, who have long been considered as rather too sufficient unto themselves.

For the manifold non-athletic interests in Dartmouth there is now a home unique among the colleges. This is Robinson Hall, the beautiful one hundred thousand dollar structure just north of College Hall. It was an inspiration of genius that prompted Wallace F. Robinson, of Boston, to the presentation of this most useful of buildings. In making the gift he thus expressed his feeling in the matter:

" Dartmouth's student organizations, with the exception of athletics, are in need of adequate quarters where their activities may be properly concentrated and efficiently controlled. As a man of affairs, with a long business experience, I believe that, suitably housed and provided with the means for the conduct of their business and for the social intercourse incidental to the activities of young men of similar tastes and abilities, these organizations would present a strong counterpoise to athleticism on the one hand, and to social cliques on the other. They would thus afford a just balance of intellectual and artistic expression as against bodily prowess and muscular skill.

" In order to insure the continued democracy of the college, I have stipulated that no organizations shall make use of the building except those in which the qualifications for membership is proved ability only."

In this clearing-house of the esthetic side of Dartmouth's student life are many mansions. No more do the college publications' staffs depend on their studies or a dingy room over some store for editorial quarters. Each has a large, handsome set of rooms, beautifully furnished — perhaps too beautifully for embryo journalists, who must some day, if they persist, have a rude awakening to the realities of real newspaper offices. There are rooms for the literary societies, for the band (cannily built at the top of the building with sound-proof walls and doors) and for the various other non-athletic organizations. There are a couple of comfortable general assembly rooms and a daintily appointed ladies' room. And in a rear extension is a lovely little theatre seating four hundred and perfectly equipped for the rehearsals and trial performances of the Dramatic Association.

Here, at Hanover, then, is the first collegiate attempt to give to student activities not connected with athletics proper recognition and encouragement by means of adequate and dignified quarters. It aims toward both the business and the social development of these organizations. Its working out will be worth the attention of all those institutions of learning in which prowess on the gridiron, or the track, or the diamond has created a species of hero-worship not always healthful to the other and certainly no less valuable activities of a student body.

CHAPTER XVI

WHY men go to any college is a question that the alumni, trustees, and faculty of each institution may best answer from their different standpoints. Why men went to Dartmouth fifty or even twenty-five years ago was no problem at all. They went mainly because Dartmouth was the only college in New Hampshire, or because their fathers or other relatives had gone there before them. None went because it was "the thing to do", and few go now for any such reason. Dartmouth has never become socially great.

But the question that was easy to answer in the iron age of the college is not so easy in the golden age. The old reasons amply accounted for an entering freshman class of sixty-five; they fail to explain the motives that bring some four hundred new candidates for entrance into the Hanoverian "groves of the academy" each year, and bring them from all parts of the United States.

Dartmouth's claim to the title of the national

college is well founded. She has more students from outside New Hampshire than has Harvard from outside Massachusetts.[1] Scores travel halfway across the continent at least twice each year for the sake of being Dartmouth men. There has been nothing more astonishing in the forward march of the college in the last twenty years than this successful appeal to the country at large. What is there in the bugle-call from the hills that is so potent in rallying young men to the green banner?

One man, Professor F. A. Updyke, freshman class officer for the college year 1912–1913, decided that an illuminating answer to the question might come from the freshmen themselves, and he instituted a poll of the three hundred and eighty-one entrants to the class of 1916. He found that of this number but seventy-five had fathers who were college graduates, and only twenty-two had fathers who had been to Dartmouth. Of the whole number eighty-three had professional men for fathers. The poll of reasons for coming to Dartmouth turned out as follows: influence of relatives in or out of college, forty-two; influence of Dartmouth graduates and undergraduates, one hundred and forty-one; location of college, forty-six; size of the college, twelve; plan of admission, eighteen; reputation and spirit

[1] The college proper is meant in each instance.

of the college, eleven; lower expense of education in Dartmouth, ten; athletics, five; Tuck School, ten; Thayer School, thirteen.

So the great propulsive force that sends men to Dartmouth is the proselyting work of Dartmouth men, both in and out of college. Nobody who has ever seen a body of Dartmouth alumni in action can doubt it. Their enthusiastic zeal in persuading boys and parents that the one place ordained by an all-wise providence as a college seat is Hanover, and that the one college worthy to occupy such a situation is Dartmouth, produces results, as the facts show.

Along these lines of endeavor the recently organized alumni council is expected to be still more productive. This organization, founded in 1913, is made up of twenty-five representatives from all parts of the country, elected by general vote of the alumni. It is to meet in conference at least once a year. Perhaps its intended province can best be expressed in the statement, that it is expected to be " a clearing-house for alumni sentiment " and a court for the approval or disapproval of alumni projects. Undoubtedly it also will devote its energies to the raising and handling of alumni funds for the college and for the maintaining of the supply and quality of its students. For this work President

WHY MEN GO TO DARTMOUTH

Emeritus Tucker has made a suggestion that might be considered radical were it not that his far-seeing wisdom has so often been triumphantly proven.

"If Dartmouth is to maintain a national constituency," says Doctor Tucker, "it must localize its constituency. Why not make Cleveland, Detroit, Omaha, Denver, and like centers permanent sources of supply? If five or six scholarships were established at each of such centers, giving sufficient income to cover tuition, at least, they would secure a steady supply of first-class and therefore influential students. Each man so provided for would bring others with him, and in time the college would come to have a recognized place in the life of the community. But to reach this result, it would be absolutely necessary to make an outright endowment of a given school or of the local board of education for this purpose. A scholarship or a system of scholarships, which might be withdrawn at pleasure, would produce little impression on a school or community. An outright endowment would give the unmistakable impression that Dartmouth was proposing to make a home for itself in that locality."

That forty-six men of a single class came to Dartmouth because of the location of the college is significant of two things: that the glories of "Dartmouth out-o'-doors " are beginning to impress themselves far and wide, and that fathers and mothers appreciate the situation of a college that has no easy access to the flashy fascinations of metropolitan evil. If a Dartmouth student wants to be " tough ", he has to make a very deliberate and inconvenient business of it. Some occasionally do just that, of course, but, says the *Alumni Magazine*, " the sooner they learn that if Dartmouth were situated five miles from Boston, it would cease to be Dartmouth, the better for them and for the college." That sentiment seems to have won favor with a quite considerable number of " the old folks at home ", who feel that as Hanover cannot be accused of turning out milksops, neither has she any ready facilities for the production of youthful " rounders."

This " magnificent isolation " is the chief glory and hope of those who rule the college — and that means the alumni of Dartmouth, as well as its trustees and faculty. President Nichols has an interesting theory that Dartmouth, and possibly Princeton, will alone, of all the larger eastern colleges, be found on their present sites five hundred years from to-day. He points out how all of the others are even now pressed hard upon by the tightening coils of industry, or commerce, or city devel-

Observatory Slope

opments, and how they are even now compelled either to tear themselves up by the roots and transplant their academic groves, or burst through their hard urban bonds and expand in some terribly costly way.

Dartmouth, on her splendid plateau, is scores of miles from any city. No stretch of the imagination, spanning even half a millennium, can picture her as beset by other interests than her own. But she is taking nothing for granted. Steadily she is acquiring outpost lands in every direction. By and by nothing can even remotely threaten her. To-day there is not a man, woman, or child in the village but is dependent in some way upon the college for a livelihood. She is the *summum bonum* of Hanover, and without her the place would revert to nature.

Thus the college is securely looking far into the ages and beginning to plan on a vast scale that is as yet but whispered, but which is impressively hinted at by the splendid new boulevard among the pine-clad ravines from the river to the campus through the great Hitchcock estate, which now gives the institution a tract from the heart of the college to the bluffs overlooking the Connecticut.

Dartmouth is frankly proclaiming her belief that she will be where she is a thousand years from now, and that she will be, as Oxford in England, almost alone in the great antiquity of her home. If that be called a vision, it is certain that it illumines many a forward-looking heart on the Hanover plain.

Some men come to Dartmouth, as has been shown by the 1912 test, because the cost of education here is relatively small. Not so many come for that reason as in the old days, but still a respectable number — perhaps more than cared to admit it in the freshman catechism. That expenses are low may be seen by the following table included in a circular sent to applicants for scholarship aid by Dean Laycock:

The college expenses put at the minimum and average may be rated as follows:

	Minimum	Average
Tuition, with college bills............	$140.	$140.
Text-books.......................	15.	30.
Instruments (if Graphics is taken) ..		12.
Laboratory fees per course (if courses are elected) $3.00...............	6.	15.
Room-rent in college building (including heat and care; room unfurnished)	50.	100.
Lights...........................	4.	6.
Board (36 weeks, $4.00–$6.00).......	140.	180.
Laundry.........................	15.	30.
	$370.	$513.

WHY MEN GO TO DARTMOUTH

Summing up this important point, an officer of the college once replied to a New York newspaper's query on the subject that: "A Dartmouth undergraduate with seven hundred dollars a year to his credit can not only go through college, but can, as well, partake of some of the joys of life in the process."

Scholarships help many, the tendency of late years being to combine them into fewer and larger ones. Intra-collegiate business enterprises fatten slender pocketbooks to some extent; a recent inquiry showed one hundred and fifty student merchants in varying degrees of prosperity. Tutoring, acting as monitors, waiting on table and working for the townspeople add to small incomes for poor men. "A student at Dartmouth", says President Nichols understandingly, "may bring food to his classmate or wash a citizen's windows without the slightest feeling of abasement on his own part or the least dulling of comradeship and respect on the part of others toward him; and this is true because there is no serving class at Hanover to which he can be compared."

The "spirit of the college" is modestly set down by our investigator of freshmen as drawing eleven men to an entering class. That may seem a small number, but it is only technically correct, for the

"Dartmouth spirit", far-famed and more clearly felt than described, is a powerful element in each of the other drawing motives, especially in that which is aroused by the work of alumni and undergraduates. In some psychological way the "Dartmouth spirit" is often impressed upon a young man before he ever sees Hanover.

Dartmouth men have been called clannish after their college lives. "They stick together", the saying is; they find jobs for the youngsters just emerging; they solidly endorse Dartmouth men for appointive offices; they even show political unity when a Dartmouth man is nominated for something or other. This sometimes vexes the onlooker, whether he be from some other college or from none. But possibly he fails to realize the power of ancestry and inheritance.

Dartmouth men were compelled to be clannish when old Eleazar's axe-wielders slashed the room for their huts and cabins out of the virgin forests of a wilderness. They were compelled to be clannish for years afterward in the hard struggle for existence. The feeling of loyalty and oneness got into the blood, and it has never gotten out. To-day the geographic aloofness of the college still works its ancient spell.

President Emeritus Tucker, than whom no man

has had better opportunity or capacity for knowing, once wrote to an inquirer on the subject:

" You ask me what I understand to be the meaning of the so-called Dartmouth spirit. If you should ask any general observer how the Dartmouth spirit differed from that of most other colleges, he would tell you, I think, that the difference was of degree more than of kind — that there was simply more of it, that it was more in evidence, more easily provoked, more irrepressible. The answer would be true, but it would only make your question more interesting. And yet there is no mystery about the Dartmouth democracy. It is the natural outgrowth of the local situation. That situation, as you know, has been practically unchanged for more than a hundred years. There have never been any dominating or disintegrating influences, political or social, at work from without upon the college community. Naturally there has grown up an unusual spirit of democracy which they found here. Probably there is no college where students are more closely related to one another, or more personally related to the college. The absence, in so large a degree, of organized and formal relations shows the reality of this underlying and almost unconscious relation. The Dartmouth democracy grows as the result of an accumulating inheritance and of a steadfast environment, especially of the latter."

Dartmouth clings to compulsory attendance at chapel every week-day morning. She surprises some other colleges in this; she is looked upon as old-fashioned, unduly orthodox, rather lagging behind in the procession of rationalism. But she knows what she is doing. That daily gathering when the whole college sees itself, feels its solidarity, looks itself over and rejoices in its strength, does more for Dartmouth loyalty and the Dartmouth spirit than any other one element that can be found in Hanover. Chapel is the only place where the whole college foregathers — for even a " big " football game has its absentees. The shouting and the tumult must, at most, be sporadic. Men may roar their " Wah-Hoo-Wahs " together and feel that the Dartmouth spirit has something to do with the game of football. But football is only thirty years old. From the day when the " Voice " first thrilled the wilderness, " Chapel " has been. It is the one existing exercise of the college that has come down from the beginning unchanged and unbroken. There is not the slightest trend toward its abolishment. Sleep-loving students may grumble at it in the customary undergraduate way; but by the time they reach senior year, they see the power and the glory of the ancient rite, and they, too, would cling to this altar of democracy, if it were threatened.

Men go to Dartmouth for many reasons, because Dartmouth has a many-sided appeal. They stay in Dartmouth because they have earned the right, and with that earning they imbibe a l   their college that challenges the admiration   n those who cannot wholly comprehend it. M   come out from Dartmouth to

> Stand as brother stands by brother!
> Dare a deed for the Old Mother!
> Greet the world, from the hills, with a hail!

No one has ever yet put into words better than those three lines the Dartmouth spirit, its staunch comradeship, its eternal devotion, and its supreme confidence. The heritage of a great past it reckons as the guardian of a greater future.

THE END

INDEX

Adams, Melvin O., 207
Ægis, 178, 261
Allen, Ethan, 66
Allen, Ira, 66
Allen, Ira B., 173
Allen, William, 101, 104, 113
Alumni Council, 270
Appleton, Samuel, 142
Armistead, Lewis Addison, 212
Arnold, Benedict, 9

Baker, William Lawrence, 163
Barron, Asa T., 173
Baseball, 247
Barstow, J. W., 134, 137, 223
Bartlett, Ichabod, 107
Bartlett, Samuel Colcord, 183, 189, 197
" Bed-bug Alley," 131, 226
Bell, Luther V., 153
Bema, The, 261
Belknap, Doctor Jeremy, 48
Bingham, Harry, 187
Bissell, George H., 180
Bissell Gymnasium, 180
Boston Packet, 1
Boston Repertory, 92
Brant, Joseph, 17
Brixam, 1
Brown, John, 154
Brown, President Francis, 97, 98, 106, 117

Brown, Reverend Francis, 5, 201, 213, 215
Brown University, 10
Bull, Ole, 233
Bunker Hill, 57
Butterfield Hall, 208
Butterfield, Ralph, 208
Burnham, Franklin James, 163
Burr, Sanford S., 152

Calvin, Hezekiah, 17
Cane rush, 225
Carter, " Lil," 235
Chamberlain, George E., 159
Chamberlain, William, 122
Chandler, Abiel, 142
Chandler Scientific Department, 142, 205
Charter of Dartmouth College, 28, 29
Chase, Salmon P., 174
Choate, Rufus, 81, 103, 106, 138
Christian Association, 264
Cleaveland, Reverend Ebenezer, 25
College cheer, 226
College Church, 90, 179
College Hall, 204
" College Party," 65, 66
College tower, 189
Commencements, 231
Concord Gazette, 93

281

INDEX

INDEX

"First sprout of the college," 34
Fletcher, Richard, 171
Football, 249
Fort Stanwix, 23
Foster, Daniel, 156
Fowler, David, 17, 18
Franklin, Benjamin, 72
Franklin, Governor, 23
Frary, "Hod," 234
French, B. F., 145
"Freshmen beer," 226
Frisbie, Levi, 41
Frost, E. B., 159
Fuller, Melville W., 213
Fullerton, William, 187

Gallagher, Charles T., 216
Gates, General, 63
Gilpatrick, Rufus, 154
Glee Club, 262
Goodrich, Chauncey, 109
Gray, Samuel, 42
"Great Awakening," 134
"Great Road," 37
Greek letter societies, 258

Haddock, Charles B., 122
Hale, Edward Everett, 213
Hancock, John, 1
Handel Society, 262
Hanover, 30
Hardy, Arthur Sherburne, 192
Harris, F. H., 243
Harvard College, 106
Hazing, 181
Henry, Patrick, 47
Hill, Isaac, 115
Hoar, George Frisbie, 213
Holmes, John, 108, 112
Hopkinson, Joseph, 108, 112, 114

"Horning," 134
Hovey, Richard, 192, 240
Howe Library, 141
Howland, Clarence, 249
Hubbard Hall, 203
Hunt, Ebenezer, 153
Huntington, Reverend Joseph, 56
Hutchins, Arthur Edwin, 160

Indian Charity School, 3, 10, 17
"Indian Thomas," 21

"Jack O'Lantern," 261
Johnson, Reverend Jacob W., 23
Johnson, J. E., 245
Johnson, Sir William, 17, 23

Keen, Robert, 7, 12
Kendrick, Ariel, 76
"Kibling's Op'ry House," 236
Kirkland, Samuel, 18

Ladd, Nathaniel Gould, 153
Lansing, Captain A. J., 26
Laws, Solomon, 132
Ledyard, John, 240
Leeds house, 81
Little, Arthur, 159
Lodge, Henry Cabot, 113
London, 1, 5
Lord, John K., 174, 201
Lord, President Nathan, 126, 127,
    130, 137, 145-149, 174
Loveland, Aaron, 81, 84

Marshall, Captain John, 1
Marshall, Chief Justice, 108
Mason, Jeremiah, 107
Massachusetts Hall, 203

283

INDEX

INDEX

Date Due